THE YOUTH BIBLE

LEADERS GUIDE

Group
Books

Loveland, Colorado

The Youth Bible Leaders Guide

Credits
Edited by Lois Keffer
Cover and interior design by Dori Walker
Illustrations contributed by Raymond Medici

Contributors: Ann Cannon, Michael Capps, Dave Carver, Karen Dockrey, Dean Feldmeyer, Amy and Mike Nappa, Jamie Snodgrass, Linda Snyder, Yvonne L.D. Steindal, Steve and Annie Wamberg, Gary Wilde, Paul Woods, Christine Yount

Library of Congress Cataloging-in-Publication Data
The Youth Bible leaders guide / [contributors Ann Cannon ... et al.].
     p.   cm.
     ISBN 1-55945-045-2
     1. Bible—Study and teaching. 2. Teenagers—Religious life.
3. Bible games and puzzles. I. Cannon, Ann.
BS600.2.Y68   1991
220'.071'2—dc20   91-35651
                                                      CIP

14 13 12 11 10 9 8 7 6 5   04 03 02 01 00 99 98 97 96 95
Printed in the United States of America.

CONTENTS

▶ Sidelight Games and Activities

INTRODUCTION

If you've put *The Youth Bible* into the hands of your kids, you've given them a marvelous tool for personal spiritual growth. The Topical Index and life-related devotions make *The Youth Bible* approachable and understandable, so kids feel comfortable studying it on their own.

Developed as a companion volume to *The Youth Bible*, this leaders guide gives you 80 meetings that will get your youth group excited about digging into God's Word. The first seven meetings provide an introduction and chronological overview to help your kids get their bearings (do you turn right or left at Ezra to get to Obadiah?).

The remaining meetings are topical, arranged alphabetically to coincide with *The Youth Bible*'s Topical Index. Each of the topics hits kids right where they live, so you can choose the study that's most appropriate to your group's needs at any given moment. And these are not your typical boring Bible studies! Group's active-learning strategies get kids involved in hands-on activities that make for memorable, life-changing learning.

The last section of this leaders guide contains more than a dozen games and activities based on the Sidelights from *The Youth Bible*. You'll appreciate this handy resource the next time you're planning an evening of fun.

So whether you want to major in the minor prophets, handle a hot topic or get together some fun and games, *The Youth Bible Leaders Guide* will be an invaluable resource. When your kids see how lively and relevant Bible study can be, they'll want to get into *The Youth Bible* on their own—which is just about the best thing that could happen!

OVERVIEW
MEETINGS

INTRODUCTION TO
THE YOUTH BIBLE

THEME: What Makes This Bible Special

The *Youth Bible* is a one-of-a-kind tool young people can use to find God's guidance for their lives. This session will introduce your kids to the unique features of *The Youth Bible* that make it accessible and helpful in dealing with real-life problems and issues.

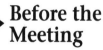 **Before the Meeting**

Obtain a copy of *The Youth Bible* for each group member. Read through the introduction to *The Youth Bible* (p. 8) and mark a few sections you feel are the most relevant to your group. Gather paper, pencils and a treat to use as a prize for activity 3, such as a candy bar or a piece of beef jerky.

 1. Getting Familiar

Pass out copies of *The Youth Bible* and give kids a few minutes to glance through it.

Ask: **What do you find interesting about this Bible? How can you see yourself using it?**

Say: **We're going to take a look at some of the unique features of this Bible and discover how we can use them to find the help we need.**

Have kids look over the introduction as you read aloud or summarize the sections you marked.

2. Fun in the Bible?

Point out the Sidelight boxes in the text of *The Youth Bible*. Give kids two or three minutes to skim through several Sidelights and have kids each choose one that especially interests them.

Let kids each read aloud their most interesting Sidelight. Then have the group vote on which was the most fun. Have the person who chose the winning Sidelight read aloud the related scripture passage.

Ask: **Did you know there were such fun things in the Bible? Do you think God has a sense of humor? What did you learn by reading these Sidelights?**

▶ 3. So That's Where That Is!

Distribute paper and pencils. Direct kids' attention to "Where Do I Find ...?" (p. 22 in *The Youth Bible*). Have kids each fold their paper in half and use it to cover the first column of scripture references.

Say: **Now look at the list of Bible characters and events. Put a checkmark on your paper by each item you could locate precisely in the Bible. Someone here is going to win a prize.**

Have kids tally their checkmarks and tell how many items they thought they could find.

Ask: **How did it feel having lots of places not checked? How might this list be helpful to us?**

Then say: **The person who wins the prize is the person with the lowest score. You get the prize because you were probably the most honest person in this group! This Bible was made for you—and for all the rest of us too!**

▶ 4. The Main Event

Say: **Now we're going to look at one of the most helpful features of this Bible—the devotions. Turn to the Topical Index on p. 11. You'll find a list of over 400 devotions on topics that relate to kids' lives today. The devotions are located in the text, near related Bible passages. These devotions aren't intended to take the place of scripture—their purpose is to help us** see how biblical principles relate to our lives.

Have kids scan the index for a topic that interests them. Let the girls vote on a topic to investigate. Then let the guys choose one of the devotions under that topic. Read through the devotion together and discuss the questions at the end. Look up the passages in the "For More, See ..." section and have kids determine what those passages can contribute to the topic.

▶ 5. Something to Consider

Have kids look at the "Consider ..." section of the devotion they discussed.

Say: **The "Consider ..." section is designed to help us put into action something we've discovered through the devotion and Bible passage.**

Form groups of about four and have kids decide how they might best put into action one of the "Consider ..." ideas. When all the groups are ready, have them report what they've chosen to do.

Say: **Action is what any Bible is all about. God doesn't intend for us to read his Word and then go away without making any changes in our lives. Let's each commit to taking action this week on what we've discussed here. Let's also commit to continuing to use *The Youth Bible* to help us find answers to our concerns.**

Close your session in prayer, thanking God for giving his Word to help us live the best lives possible.

THE BEGINNING

THEME: Genesis—Deuteronomy

A sense of purpose is important to teenagers. What kids perceive about their motivations and expectations has a great impact on their self-image. This meeting will help your kids see that God works through people who are willing to commit their lives to him. It will challenge them to rid their lives of obstacles that stand in the way of wholeheartedly serving the Lord.

▶ Before the Meeting

Prepare enough comic books or old magazines for all your kids by tearing out the first page of every story or article. You'll also need a copy of *The Youth Bible* for each group member, more popped popcorn than your kids can eat, newsprint or a chalkboard, a marker, two toothbrushes, slips of paper, and a wastebasket or preparations for a small fire.

▶ 1. No Beginnings

As kids arrive, pass out the comic books or magazines you've prepared. Encourage kids to read quietly as others arrive. If kids complain about the missing pages, just put them off by saying something like, "Oh, don't worry about the pages that are missing; just enjoy what's there."

After all the kids have had a chance to read some of the books, ask: **How did you like the** books? What was wrong with them? Why did it make a difference that the beginnings of the stories were missing? How is reading these books like trying to study the Bible without studying the first books in it?

Say: **Today we're going to be looking at the earliest history given us in the Bible, starting with Creation in Genesis. And we're going to learn what all of that has to do with us.**

▶ 2. The Beginnings on Film

Form three groups. If you have more than 18 kids, form more groups in multiples of three. Assign each group one of the following books: Genesis (p. 1), Exodus (p. 57) or Deuteronomy (p. 160). Have groups each read the introduction of their book and skim through the headings of the sections in *The Youth Bible*.

Then say: **You've all just become movie**

producers. You're going to make a movie based on your book. Choose a title for the movie, make up descriptions of three exciting scenes from the book, and prepare one of those scenes to act out for everyone else. You've got 15 minutes.

After the 15 minutes, pass out popcorn for kids to munch. Have groups each give their title for their movie, describe two of their three scenes and act out the other one.

Then ask the following questions, writing kids' answers on a chalkboard or on newsprint: **What are important things to remember about Genesis? Exodus? Deuteronomy? How did God work in or through the people in these books? What principles for living can we draw from the scenes acted out or described?**

3. Popcorn Applications

Form two lines, with kids facing each other about six feet apart. Each person should have a partner directly across from him or her. Give kids each 10 pieces of popcorn.

Say: **Your object is to try to toss your pieces of popcorn into the mouth of the person across from you. But before you throw a piece of popcorn, you must look at the list of ideas we've come up with from the Bible and tell one direct application we can make to our lives.**

Have partners alternate throwing and catching the popcorn as they make applications of the Bible principles. Award toothbrushes to the pair who catches the most kernels.

4. The Choice Is Yours

Have a volunteer read aloud Deuteronomy 30:19-20, part of Moses' last speech to the people of Israel.

Then say: **God's given each of us a choice. Either we follow his principles and apply them to our lives, or we choose to ignore him.**

Pass out slips of paper and ask kids to write on their papers what might be keeping them from making a full commitment to God. Give kids a couple of minutes to think and write.

If it's possible to go to a place where you can start a small fire, take kids there to wrap up this session. If it's not possible, have kids gather around a wastebasket and tear up their slips of paper.

Say: **Thousands of years ago, Moses stood at the burning bush and decided to give his life to God. Now, as you throw your papers into the fire (or the wastebasket), let your actions stand for getting rid of any obstacles that stand in the way of committing your life fully to God. Ask God to help you follow through on applying to your life the principles we've talked about today.**

Close your session with prayer, asking God to help each of your kids get past their obstacles to serving him.

BEING FAITHFUL

THEME: Leviticus—Esther

It's not easy to be a Christian teenager in today's world. It wasn't easy to follow God faithfully in Old Testament times either. The Israelites struggled and often failed. But sometimes they rejoiced in the fellowship with God that comes with faithful obedience. Your kids can learn from the Israelites that God will be there to help them stay true if they continue to depend on him.

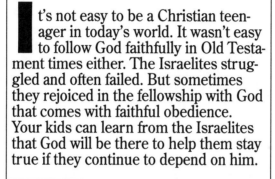

▶ Before the Meeting

Prepare enough slips of paper for all your kids to have one. On half of the slips write, "No thanks, I don't like that kind." On the other half write, "Thanks, I'd love one." You'll need enough cookies for the whole group. Write the questions from activity 2 on newsprint or a chalkboard. You'll need a copy of *The Youth Bible* for each group member.

▶ 1. How Hard It Is

Choose an outgoing, confident person to leave the room. Then pass out the slips of paper you've prepared. Tell kids to respond with what's written on their slip, no matter what the person outside the room says to them.

Have the person outside the room return and give him or her the cookies to distribute, with instructions to make sure everyone gets a cookie.

After the fun and the arguing have stopped,

tell everyone they can ignore their slips and have cookies if they want.

Then ask: **How did you feel if you couldn't take a cookie? How hard was it to stay faithful to the instructions on your paper when the cookies were offered? How is this like staying faithful to God when others around you are ignoring him?**

Say: **After God brought the people of Israel out of slavery in Egypt, he began to shape them into his people. But they didn't always follow him. They often messed up— just like we do sometimes. Today we're going to take a look at some of their mistakes and some of the good things they did in trying to stay faithful to God.**

▶ 2. Revealing Research

Form four groups (a group can be as small as one person). Assign groups each one of the following sections: Leviticus—Joshua;

Judges—2 Samuel; 1 Kings—2 Chronicles; Ezra—Esther. Have each group choose a scribe and give each of the scribes a pencil and paper.

Say: **You're writing a major research paper for an ancient history course. You've decided to examine why the Israelites survived as a people when many other nations have disappeared from the earth. Read through the introductions to your books and use the information to answer these questions. Some books may be more helpful than others.**

Post these questions on a sheet of newsprint.
● What struggles did the Israelites have?
● What did they do to stay faithful to God?
● What good things happened to them?
● In what ways did God work to help them?

Give kids about 15 minutes for their research. When groups are finished, let them give oral reports on their research projects.

Ask: **Did the Israelites always stay faithful to God? Explain. Did God remain faithful? Explain. When did things go best for the people?**

▶ **3. Faithfulness Defined**

Have someone read aloud Joshua 24:14-15.
Ask: **What does it mean for us to serve the Lord faithfully today?**
Form groups of three or four. Within each group, have kids discuss specific ways teenagers can serve God. Then work together as a whole group to write your own definition of a faithful teenager.

▶ **4. As for Me . . .**

Say: **After Joshua said the words we read just a few minutes ago, the Israelites responded to him. Let's look at their response.**
Have kids look up Joshua 24:16-18. Ask someone to read it aloud.
Ask: **What help did the Israelites have in staying true to God? Can we depend on that same help? Why or why not?**
Gather kids in a circle.
To wrap up your session, say: **I'm going to give you a chance to make the same commitment to God the Israelites did. I'll issue the same challenge, and those of you who want to will respond with the last part of Joshua 24:18—"We will continue to serve the Lord because he is our God."**
Say: **You must choose for yourselves today. You must decide whom you will serve . . . As for me and my family, we will serve the Lord.**
Let kids respond, then close with prayer that kids will rely on God to help them keep the commitments they've made.

HONORING GOD

THEME: Job—Song of Solomon

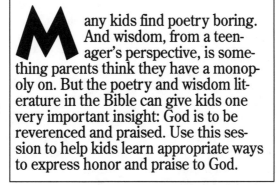

Many kids find poetry boring. And wisdom, from a teenager's perspective, is something parents think they have a monopoly on. But the poetry and wisdom literature in the Bible can give kids one very important insight: God is to be reverenced and praised. Use this session to help kids learn appropriate ways to express honor and praise to God.

▶ Before the Meeting

Find an example of poetry to read for activity 1. You'll need paper, pencils and copies of *The Youth Bible* for everyone.

▶ 1. Poetic Justice?

Open your session by reading one of your favorite poems. Choose any style you like—something that appeals to your taste, not necessarily to the taste of the kids in your group. If you have difficulty choosing a poem, use a nursery rhyme or a selection from a book of Mother Goose.

After you've read the poetry, ask: **Wasn't that fine poetry?**

After the laughter or the boos die down, ask: **What's your favorite poetry?**

Challenge kids to recite any poetry they can remember. You may have to prime them with some nursery rhymes if you didn't use them for your first example. When kids seem to have run out of poetry they remember, start quoting or reading the 23rd Psalm. Encourage anyone who knows parts of it to say it along with you.

Then say: **You may not have realized that much of the Old Testament, including Psalms, is made up of Hebrew poetry. The words don't rhyme like they sometimes do in our poetry, but they often have a specific rhythm and repeat similar thoughts in consecutive lines. Today we're going to be looking at some of the poetry in the Bible and also at a section of scripture we call wisdom literature.**

▶ 2. Poetic Themes

Say: **The books of Job, Psalms, Proverbs, Ecclesiastes and Song of Solomon are known as poetry and wisdom literature. Let's look at what *The Youth Bible* has to** say about each of these books.

Form two groups. Pass out paper and pencils. Assign Job (p. 451) and Psalms (p. 481) to one group, and Proverbs (p. 567), Ecclesiastes (p. 597) and Song of Solomon (p. 608) to the other. Have groups read the introductions to their books and skim through the pages to get ready to report on these three things: one theme in the book, how God is referred to in the book and one helpful principle in the book.

Give kids about 10 minutes to research and prepare, then have each group report its findings.

Say: **See how helpful poetry can be? Let's look more specifically at some of the poetry in these books.**

3. Poetry in Music

Form five groups (a group can be just one person). Assign each group one of the following passages: Job 12:5-16; Psalm 103:1-13; Proverbs 2:1-8; Ecclesiastes 12:11-14; Song of Solomon 2:11-13.

Have groups each read their poetry passage and choose what they feel is the most important part of it. Then have them reword that section and set it to the tune of a familiar song. Bring everyone together and have groups perform their songs.

After the concert, ask: **What attitudes about God or his creation did each of these passages show? Do you think God is pleased with the reverence and praise of these books? Explain. How can we best reverence and honor God?**

Give kids a few minutes to discuss and apply the last question before moving on to the next activity.

4. Reflecting Pool

Say: **The 23rd Psalm tells us that the Lord makes us lie down by still waters. Sometimes it's good to look into those still waters and reflect. We're going to spend the next three minutes browsing through the book of Psalms and reflecting on all God has done for us. Let's have a reverent silence as we stop and think about how awesome our God is.**

Three minutes can be a long time for kids to be silent, but don't cut it short. When the time is up, give volunteers a few minutes to tell what they discovered.

5. Make a Joyful Noise!

Say: **Much of the poetry in the Bible was written to be sung, just as we did a few minutes ago. Now let's write our own song of praise to God.**

Let kids choose the tune of a favorite worship chorus for their song. Then have each group from activity 3 suggest one or two lines for the song. Work as a group to put all the lines together so they form a meaningful verse.

Sing your song together as a closing prayer of worship and praise.

THE PROPHETS

THEME: Isaiah—Malachi

The prophets were God's messengers. They "told it like it was" at times when God's truth was desperately needed—sometimes for hope, sometimes for correction. When their frank reporting of God's message brought ridicule and rough treatment, the prophets hung in there, realizing that their message was the lifeline between a lost world and a loving God.

Christian teenagers who care about sharing God's truth for today may face the same kind of reception the prophets did. This meeting will challenge your kids to keep on telling others about God's messages for our time, even in the face of negative reactions.

▶ Before the Meeting

Tape up a whole roll of shelf paper around the walls of your meeting room. Hide a snack (like a pizza cut in bite-sized pieces) in a nearby room. Gather a whistle; cotton balls; two or three bottles of children's bubbles; empty paper towel tubes; wide-tipped markers in red, blue and black; a roll of tape; and several pairs of scissors. Make sure there are enough copies of *The Youth Bible* for everyone.

▶ 1. Conflict of Interest

Ask for a few volunteers to be "messengers." Take them outside the room and explain where you've hidden the food in a nearby room. Their task is to lead the other kids to the food by saying: "Follow me! The end is near!" They may not touch anyone, but they may use any other method to convince the rest of the group to follow them to the food.

Now send the "messengers" out in the hallway. Tell them they can come back into the room and start spreading their message when they hear you blow your whistle.

Call the rest of the kids together and tell them that when you blow your whistle, they are to stare at the ceiling and whistle "Yankee Doodle." Give them cotton balls to put in their ears and explain that they are not to allow anything to distract them from their task until you blow the whistle a second time.

Now blow your whistle to call the messengers back into the larger group. It will be interesting to see the antics of the messengers as they try to convince the whistlers to follow them to the food. Blow the whistle after a couple of minutes.

Ask the messengers: **How did you feel when you were trying to convince these people to follow you?**

Ask the whistlers: **How did you feel about the messengers? Did you understand that they were trying to lead you to pizza, and that if you didn't hurry it would be all gone? Is anybody interested in having that pizza now?**

Have the messengers deliver the pizza to the rest of the group.

As kids eat, ask: **How was the feeling you had as messengers similar to how the Old Testament prophets might have felt?**

Say: **The Old Testament prophets had an important message to deliver but nobody wanted to listen. The prophets felt frustrated, threatened and angry. But God had given them an important job to do, and they kept at it.**

▶ 2. Here I Am!

Have your students examine Isaiah 6:1-8 and plan ways to dramatize the action. Ask for two volunteers to be the narrator and to mime the role of Isaiah. Have groups of three work together to create the six-winged heavenly creatures. A special effects crew can wave children's bubble wands to create "smoke," beat their feet on the floor to shake the walls of the temple, and speak in unison through paper towel tubes to imitate the voice of God.

Make the production as elaborate as the kids desire, emphasizing the awesome holiness of the experience. You may wish to videotape it.

After your production, ask: **What words would you use to describe Isaiah's feelings during these events? What made him feel this way? How would you feel if something like this happened to you today? Do you think it would change your life? In what way?**

Say: **The prophets took their calling from God quite seriously, and no wonder. Hearing from God up-close and in person is pretty big stuff! Let's take a look at the Old Testament prophets as a group and check out what they heard from God and what they had to say.**

▶ 3. Stand and Deliver

There are 17 books in the Old Testament "prophet section": Isaiah, Jeremiah, Lamentations, Ezekiel, Daniel, Hosea, Joel, Amos, Obadiah, Jonah, Micah, Nahum, Habbakuk, Zephaniah, Haggai, Zechariah and Malachi. Divide the books between groups of kids and assign each group a section of the shelf paper "scroll" you've taped to the wall. Unless your youth group is large, you probably won't want to cover all the prophets. Have the groups look in *The Youth Bible* at the introduction to each of the books they've been assigned.

Say: **Divide your wall "scroll" into sections—one section for each of the prophets you're looking up. Then do three things for each prophet.**
1. **Write the names of these "true blue" guys with blue marker.**
2. **Find out what their main urgent message was and write it in red marker.**
3. **Write in plain black and white what you think they would have to say to people today.**

Encourage kids to look for some interesting details of the prophets' lives as they do their research. When the groups have finished, call them together in the center of the room.

Ask: **What similarities do you see in the messages? What are the differences? What message do you think your school needs to hear most? Your family? This group?**

Say: **God still uses people today to carry his message. Maybe this week you could let God use you.**

▶ 4. That's a Wrap!

Give each group a pair of scissors and a piece of tape. Have them cut down their section of the wall scroll and wrap it around their group members. Tape the ends together if possible.

Say: **Walking around with important messages from the Bible taped to your bodies is one way to draw people's attention to what God's Word has to say—but it's probably not the most efficient way. Before we** "break" (literally) today, I want each group to tell me how it's going to get its message out to the people who need to hear it.

After kids have shared their ideas, have them "explode" out of their scroll wrapper. Say: **Take some pieces of your group's scroll with you as a reminder to get God's message out to those around you.**

5. Prophetically Speaking

Close by gathering kids in a circle. Have them name some positive characteristics of the prophets such as courage, honesty and persistence. Then have them each turn to the person on their left and say, "I think God has given you some of the prophets' (insert a characteristic) to help you speak for him."

To close, lead in a prayer asking God to help each of the kids carry his message in actions and words this week.

THE LIFE OF CHRIST

THEME: Matthew—John

Ask your kids about a popular rock star, and they'll rattle off information ranging from album sales to the star's favorite flavor of ice cream. But media stars enjoy only fleeting moments of fame and influence. By giving an overview of the gospels, this session will expose kids to facts about a "celebrity" who's around to stay, the most significant person who ever walked the planet—Jesus Christ.

▶ Before the Meeting

Make a photocopy of the "4×4×2 Road Rally" for every two kids.

Gather pencils, modeling clay, a small squirt gun and copies of *The Youth Bible*.

▶ 1. Ten Questions

Play a variation of the standard "20 Questions" parlor game. Ask a volunteer to think of a famous person and to keep the identity of the person a secret. You may want to know the identity of the person to help the game along. The rest of the group can ask a total of 10 yes-or-no questions, with one guess of the person's identity after each question. If the group hasn't guessed the "mystery person" after 10 questions, have the volunteer reveal it.

Play a few rounds of the game, then ask: **How did you feel when you didn't have the slightest idea who the mystery person was? How did it feel when you realized you were hot on the trail? What did all the people you guessed have in common? What makes people famous? Do you always believe what you hear in the media about famous people? Explain.**

Say: **One of the most talked about people in history is Jesus Christ. His life shouldn't be a mystery to anyone. Today, we're going to look at the four gospels to get an overview of Jesus' life and rediscover why he is unique in history.**

▶ 2. Just the Facts

Ask the kids to turn to John 20:30-31. Read the verses aloud.

Then ask: **Why did John write this book? If you were hearing about Jesus for the** first time, what kinds of things would help you believe that Jesus is "the Christ, the Son of God"?

Say: **Jesus' life on earth was truly amazing—unique in all history. This handout will help you discover or review some of the highlights of Jesus' life and ministry.**

Have kids find partners. Give each pair a copy of the "4×4×2 Road Rally" handout.

Say: **It's cruisin' time. You and your partner will find the information you need to finish the road rally in the introductions to the four gospels as well as in the gospels themselves. The subheads in** *The Youth Bible* **will help you locate facts and information.**

If your kids are fairly equal in Bible skills, you may choose to make this a timed event. When the handouts are completed, have kids compare their responses.

Then ask: **Which of the items you listed would be most influential in helping people believe that Jesus is the son of God? What impresses you about the miracles of Jesus? the places he went? the people he spent time with?**

 ## 3. CommuniClay

Give kids each a lump of modeling clay.

Say: **Use this clay to create a sculpture that illustrates something that's important to you about who Jesus is or what he did on earth.**

After a few minutes, ask kids to share their "works of art."

Ask: **What was difficult about this project? What new insights about Jesus occurred to you as you were working? How was expressing your thoughts about Jesus in clay like trying to tell others about who he is?**

 ## 4. Squirting Facts

Gather the group in a circle.

Pull out a small squirt gun and say: **Somebody's going to get wet. When I squirt the gun, I'm also going to "squirt out" a fact about Jesus. The person I squirt will squirt someone else, and tell another fact about Jesus. When we're all wet, we're all done!**

Close the session by going around the circle, having kids say to the person on their right, "By believing, you can have life through his name."

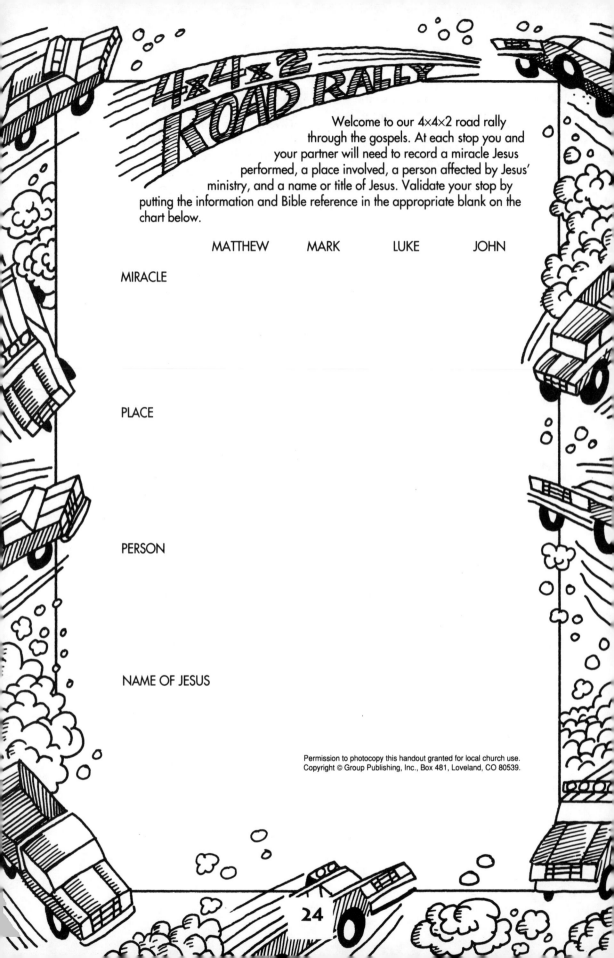

4×4×2 ROAD RALLY

Welcome to our 4×4×2 road rally through the gospels. At each stop you and your partner will need to record a miracle Jesus performed, a place involved, a person affected by Jesus' ministry, and a name or title of Jesus. Validate your stop by putting the information and Bible reference in the appropriate blank on the chart below.

	MATTHEW	MARK	LUKE	JOHN
MIRACLE				
PLACE				
PERSON				
NAME OF JESUS				

THE FIRST CHRISTIANS

THEME: Acts—Revelation

Pioneers chart unknown territory. They trade security for adventure to build and settle where no one has gone before. This session will help your kids see the first Christians as pioneers whose faithfulness in following God established the church for future generations.

▶ **Before the Meeting**

Set up the "Who's Up First?" table described in activity 1. Gather three cardboard boxes, a candy bar, a soft drink, a small pail of confetti, markers, masking tape, paper and pencils and large balloons. Make sure you have copies of *The Youth Bible* for everyone.

▶ **1. Who's Up First?**

Set up a table with three cardboard boxes hiding three items. Put a candy bar under the first box, a soft drink under the second and a bucket of confetti under the third. Don't let kids see what's under the boxes.

Say: **I need three volunteers who are willing to take whatever's under these three boxes.**

Stand behind the boxes and call up one volunteer at a time. Ask each volunteer how he or she feels right before lifting the box. Have the first two volunteers uncover the candy bar and the soft drink. When the third box is lifted, shower the volunteer with confetti.

Ask the volunteers: **What made you decide to participate in this activity? How did you feel just before you lifted your box? What risks are involved in being among the first to do something new? What risks do you think were involved in being among the first followers of Christ?**

Say: Today we're going to look at the books of the Bible that tell the story and the teachings of the first Christians. We'll discover the challenges they faced as pioneers of the faith.

▶ **2. Learning to Build**

Tell kids to turn to Ephesians 2:20-22. Read the passage aloud.

Ask: **What attitudes would the early Christians need in order to allow God to** build them together?

Form four groups (a group can be only one person). Assign the 23 books of the New Testament that deal with the early church among the groups as follows: (1) Acts—Galatians; (2) Ephesians—2 Timothy; (3) Titus—2 Peter; (4) 1 John—Revelation.

Give each group a marker and as many balloons as it has books. Have groups look in the introduction of each assigned book for one teaching or characteristic that would have helped the first Christians be built together as God's church. For each book, groups will blow up a balloon, tie it off, and write on it the name of the book and the teaching or characteristic they discovered.

After all the groups have covered their assigned material and prepared their balloons, have them work together to assemble a balloon building by connecting the balloons with masking tape. As groups connect their balloons to the building, have them tell the others the name of the book the balloon represents and explain the importance of the teaching or characteristic they found in it.

When the building is complete, ask: **How did it feel working together to build this balloon building? How are those feelings like the feelings the early Christians might have had as they worked together?**

As we look over these books of the Bible, do you notice any recurring elements that helped build the church? What do you think might have been toughest for the first Christians to learn? Which of these teachings would most benefit our local church? Which of these characteristics do you see demonstrated among Christians today?

▶ **3. The Fish Marks the Spot**

Draw a fish symbol on a sheet of newsprint.

Say: **One thing the first Christians shared was a secret code: the mark of the fish. They'd scratch it in the ground with a stick** to identify themselves to other Christians. **One person would draw one arc of the fish. If the other person was a Christian, he or she would finish the symbol by drawing the other arc. Christians also used the fish sign to mark the way to meeting places, especially in cities where there was severe persecution.**

Ask: **Does anyone know the significance of the fish, or *icthus*, and how it came to be used as a Christian symbol?**

You may need to explain that the word "*icthus*" means fish in Greek. *Icthus* is an acronym, using the first letters of the phrase, "Jesus Christ, God's Son, Savior." The acronym looks like this:

I = Jesus
C = Christ
TH = God's
U = Son
S = Savior.

Have kids find partners. Ask one partner from each pair to leave the room. The remaining kids will take a small piece of masking tape, make the mark of the fish on it, initial it and hide it somewhere in the room. Then have them come to the center of the room and stand in a tight circle facing out.

Call in the other partners. Explain that their goal is to find their partners' fish marks. The partners who did the hiding will coach by saying "hot" or "cold" to indicate when the searchers are getting closer or farther away. But the coaches may not move—they have to call their directions from their circle in the center of the room.

After all the fish marks are found, ask: **How did it feel trying to give directions? How did it feel trying to follow your partner's directions? How are those feelings similar to the way the early Christians might have felt as they tried to follow God's leading in pioneering the Christian faith? What distractions did the first Christians need to overcome? What distracts Christians today from following God's leading in their lives?**

▶ 4. Pioneers

Distribute paper and pencils.

Say: **The first Christians faced a lot of uncertainty. Still, they faithfully followed the Holy Spirit's leading and allowed God to build them together into his church. You can be a pioneer, too, by allowing God to lead you in new expressions of faith.**

Ask: **What can you do to help build God's church—as an individual or as a group?**

Have kids work with their partners from activity 3 to brainstorm and make a quick sketch of a pioneering project to help build the church. Let partners share their ideas with the whole group.

Close in prayer, thanking God for the brave faith of the early Christians and asking his help for the same willingness to follow the Spirit's leading today.

TOPICAL MEETINGS

TICKED OFF

THEME: Anger

Attitudes about anger range from viewing it as always sinful to prescribing that it be fully vented at every opportunity. Help your kids recognize that anger is a normal, healthy reaction to certain situations of attack, shame and frustration. But help them also see that they always have a choice in the way they express their angry feelings—either destructively or constructively.

▶ Before the Meeting

Gather a length of rope, a sponge, a butter knife, a rubber mallet and a roll of strong tape. You'll also need paper, pencils, newsprint and markers. Make sure everyone has a copy of *The Youth Bible*.

▶ 1. Helpful or Harmful?

Form five groups. (A group can be one person.) Give each group one of the common household objects listed above.

Give the groups five minutes to come up with two short skits using their object as a prop. The first skit will show how that object could be used as a destructive "weapon" in a situation of anger or rage. The other skit will show how the same object could be used in a constructive way to help others. For example, a length of rope could be used to strangle someone, or it could be used to pull someone to safety.

After the skits, bring the groups together and ask: **How hard was it to think of a destructive use for these objects? How hard was it to think of a helpful use for them? Which seems to be easier in your experience: reacting destructively in anger or finding a way to use anger for good? Explain.**

▶ 2. Anger Memos

Have kids return to their groups. Assign each group one of the following devotions and passages in *The Youth Bible*: "One Mad Mom," 2 Chronicles 36:14-21; "Jealous Anger," Nahum 1:2-6; "Beating the Bully," Matthew 5:17-26; "Constructive Anger," John 2:12-22; and "Handle with Care," Ephesians 4:25—5:2. Give each group a sheet of paper and a pencil.

Say: **Each of your groups is going to produce a business memo. The memo will state a principle based on your scripture passage that could help a teenager deal** with a real-life, anger-producing situation. You can address the memo to a specific imaginary figure who got mad and blew up, or to everyone who ever gets angry.

Let the kids know they can "ham it up" with the stilted language style often found in business memos. Show them a typical memo format you've created on newsprint to get them started.

After groups have composed their memos, have them each appoint a spokesperson to read and explain the memo to the whole group, telling how it relates to the scripture passage.

Ask: **Is it a sin to be angry? Explain. How would you summarize the Bible's basic approach to anger? What is the best way to respond to anger? How can we acknowledge and vent our anger without sinning?**

Say: **We can't help feeling angry sometimes. Often we have legitimate reasons for being ticked off. And no amount of saying to ourselves, "I shouldn't feel this way," is going to make us feel different. But we do have choices about how we will use our anger: We can channel angry energy into actions of destruction, or we can put that anger to work by doing something to bring about positive change in the situation. Let's look at three situations that illustrate this point.**

▶ 3. Real-Life Rage

Have kids turn to the devotion "Rage" (p. 1110 in *The Youth Bible*). Use the three vignettes as mini-case studies for discussion. Read the story of Ann aloud.

Ask: **Why did Ann's anger build up to the point of violence? What things could have** prevented that buildup? What are other ways Ann could've handled her anger?

Next read the story of Alan aloud.

Ask: **Did Alan solve his acceptance problems? Will people respect him now? Explain.**

Finally, read the story of Stephen aloud, along with Acts 7:54-60.

Ask: **Should Stephen have tried to run away? Was it worth it to submit to others' rage in this situation? Was this Stephen's only choice? Explain.**

▶ 4. Holy Alternatives

Have kids turn to the devotion "Handle With Care" (p. 1223 in *The Youth Bible*). Distribute paper and pencils and lead kids in the first "Consider ..." activity. Tell kids to create two columns on their papers, one titled "Things That Make Me Angry" and the other titled "Action Without Sin."

Allow time for kids to fill in their columns in silence, then ask for volunteers to share some of their responses. Affirm kids in their attempts to find practical, positive solutions to their anger-producing situations.

▶ 5. Face-to-Face Exhortations

Have kids sit in a circle and bow in silence as you read aloud Psalm 4. After the reading, repeat the phrase in verse 4: "When you are angry, do not sin." Say to the person on your left: **(Name), in your anger do not sin.** Have kids continue this exhortation around the circle.

Close the session with a brief prayer for God's strength to handle anger in his way.

RECIPE FOR SUCCESS

THEME: Bible Study

A lot of kids spell Bible study B-O-R-I-N-G. No one will deny that it's a real challenge to maintain consistent Bible study habits, even for mature Christians. This meeting will help your kids see that daily Bible study is a privilege—not a "have to"—and a very important part of a Christian's "recipe for success."

▶ Before the Meeting

Gather a recipe, the ingredients and the utensils for making peanut butter cookies. Arrange to have the opening part of the meeting in or near a kitchen. Use different-color markers to write out these scripture references on sheets of plastic food wrap: Deuteronomy 6:2-3; Joshua 1:8; and 2 Timothy 3:16. Then cut the sheets of plastic wrap into six to eight pieces to form puzzles.

You'll also need sunglasses, a stopwatch or watch with a second hand, paper, envelopes, markers and copies of *The Youth Bible*.

▶ 1. Gooky Cookies

Have kids form two groups. Give each group a mixing bowl, a cookie sheet and the ingredients for peanut butter cookies. But give only one group a recipe. Have both groups mix up a batch of cookies. The group without a recipe may be hesitant to try to "wing it"—just encour-age the kids to give it their best shot.

As the cookies bake, ask: **How did you feel about trying to make cookies without a recipe? How do you think the "no-recipe cookies" will turn out? How is making cookies without a recipe like trying to live for God without studying the Bible?**

Say: **Kids give a lot of reasons for** *not* **studying the Bible. In this meeting we're going to look at some of the** *benefits* **of spending time in God's Word each day.**

▶ 2. Puzzle Wrap

Have kids form three groups. Wad up the three plastic wrap puzzles and give one to each group. Because of the nature of the plastic wrap, it'll be a challenge for kids to tell whether a puzzle piece is facing up or down.

Say: **On the word "go" I want you to put your puzzle together, then look up the Bible passage that's written on it. When** you all have your Bibles open to your verse, stand up and yell, "We've got it!"

Have volunteers read their group's passage aloud.

Ask: **How did it feel trying to put your puzzle together when you didn't know which side was up and which side was down? How is that like trying to live your life without the help of the Bible? According to these verses, what benefits do you think you personally can receive from studying the Bible? What things get in the way of reading the Bible on a consistent basis? How is reading the Bible like putting together a puzzle?**

Read aloud "Putting the Pieces Together" (p. 1118 in *The Youth Bible)* and have kids discuss the questions at the end.

▶ 3. Lights On

Ask a volunteer to read "Where's Your Focus?" (p. 196 in *The Youth Bible*). Have kids discuss the questions.

Then put on a pair of sunglasses and say: **Tim was hiding his music listening habits from the light of God's Word. What other habits sometimes come in conflict with God's standards?**

Say: **I'm going to pass these sunglasses around. Each person will wear them for 10 seconds. As you put them on, I want you to think about areas of your life you might be hiding from the truth God shows us in his Word. When I call time, pass the sunglasses to the next person. As you take the sunglasses off, open those hidden areas to God's truth and light.**

If your group is larger than 12, form groups of six to eight for this activity, and provide a pair of sunglasses for each group.

▶ 4. A Word From Your Sponsor

Form groups of three or more and assign each group one of the following passages: Psalm 19; 2 Timothy 3:14—4:5; and James 1:17-27.

Say: **Read through your Bible passage and the devotion that goes with it. Then use what you've learned to make up a commercial encouraging other kids to get into daily Bible study.**

Allow a few minutes of preparation time, then have groups each present their commercial.

Ask: **Of all the things we've mentioned today, what motivates you personally to study God's Word?**

▶ 5. No Excuses

Ask someone to read aloud 2 Peter 1:16-21 and the accompanying devotion, "God's Love Letter."

Ask: **How many of you have ever written or received a "love note"? How do you think you would react if you received one? What would you do with the note?**

Say: **When we think of the Bible as God's personal love letter to us, it makes the reading exciting. Today I'm going to give you a chance to respond to God's "love letter" with a love letter of your own. In your letter tell God what excuses you've used in the past for not reading his Word. Then make a "no excuses" pledge with a concrete plan for Bible study that you'll begin to carry out this week.**

Give kids envelopes for their letters. Have them each write the date one month from today on their envelope. Explain that on that date, they are to open their envelopes to check up on how they're doing with their Bible study plans.

Close the meeting by sharing the peanut butter cookies kids made at the beginning of the session. Compare the cookies made with a recipe and those made without one.

BRAG BUSTERS

THEME: Bragging

It's hard not to spot a braggart—strutting through the lunchroom after making first string on the football team, plopping the straight-A report card on top of a stack of books for everyone to see, or peeling out of the school parking lot. All bragging stems from a fundamental need to be loved and accepted—a need all kids have, everywhere, all the time. This meeting will help kids break the bragging cycle and show them how to turn their bragging energy toward encouraging others.

▶ Before the Meeting

Hang several rolls of Life Savers candies with string a few inches from the ceiling. Gather paper, tape, yarn, markers, pencils and construction paper. Make sure everyone has a copy of *The Youth Bible*.

▶ 1. Towering Achievements

As kids arrive, give them each two or three sheets of plain white paper and a marker. Have more paper, tape, and 2- to 3-foot pieces of yarn available on a nearby table.

Have kids think of things they've done that give them a sense of pride; for example, being in the marching band, making a decent grade in a difficult course, or landing a part in the school play. Kids will write each of their achievements on separate sheets of paper, then tape the papers together to form a tower.

Next have kids tape loops of yarn to the top of their "towering achievements" and stand on chairs to hang the towers from the ceiling with tape. When all the towers are hanging, have kids walk around the room and examine each other's work.

After a minute or two, call everyone together and ask: **How did it feel to create a tower with your achievements? How did it feel to have others look at your tower?**

Say: **It may be a little embarrassing to show off our accomplishments, but deep down most of us want others to know what we've done so they'll like us.**

▶ 2. Buddy Boosters

Have kids take down their towers, then say: **Sometimes our desire for people to like us leads to bragging. The problem is that bragging makes people like you less, not more. Nobody likes it when people "toot their own horns." Let's play a quick game**

35

to help us see how bragging affects others.

Tell kids that on your signal, they are to form groups and try to grasp with their teeth one of the Life Savers rolls you hung from the ceiling. They may not use any props except their bodies. Some kids will pair up, others will gather in larger groups, and still others may be left out of a group altogether. That's okay. Just let the groups form naturally.

When one group finally gets a roll of Life Savers, call a halt to the game and congratulate the winners.

Then ask: **How did it feel to be the first one to get the candy? How did it feel to be left out? What would you say is the secret to getting the candy as fast as possible?**

Retrieve all the candy rolls, and distribute Life Savers to everyone. Say: **It's easy for us to try to out-do each other, then brag about our accomplishments. But as you can tell from this game, going it alone isn't the best way to reach your goals. We all need each other's help and encouragement.**

▶ 3. Bible Braggarts

Form four groups (a group may be one person), and assign each group one of these devotions and passages from *The Youth Bible*: "She Spoke Too Soon," 1 Samuel 2:1-10; "A Tale of Two Teenagers," Luke 1:39-56; and "Cliff-hangers," Luke 12:13-21; or "Spain's Greatest Matador . . . Almost," James 3:13-18.

Have groups each read their passage and devotion, then prepare a role-play of their devotion to perform for the whole group.

After each group presents its role-play, ask: **Who has the problem with bragging in this story? How did the bragging affect others? How does your passage apply to the story? From this passage, how do you think God feels about bragging?**

After all the role-plays, read aloud Genesis

11:1-9 to the whole group.

Ask: **How is the tower in this passage like the towers you created at the start of the meeting?**

Say: **Like the people in this passage, when we try to measure ourselves by our own accomplishments, we always fall short of God's best for us. But by using Christ as our standard and loving each other, we can become all that God wants us to be.**

▶ 4. Tower Two

Say: **As a sign of our commitment not to brag and to build each other up, let's practice affirming the good things we see in each other.**

Distribute construction paper and pencils. One by one, have group members take turns standing in the center of the room. The rest of the kids will write at least two things they admire about the person in the center, using a separate sheet of paper for each comment.

When all the kids have received affirmations, have them use the affirmation sheets to build towers similar to those in the first activity.

Then ask: **How are your feelings about this tower different from your feelings about the first tower you built? What does this activity tell you about the effects of bragging versus the effects of encouraging others?**

▶ 5. Circle of Thanks

Pile all the towers from activity 4 in the center of the room and have kids form a circle around them.

Close with prayer, thanking God for all the praiseworthy things he's placed in each of us, and asking him to help us to encourage others rather than brag about ourselves.

LET'S CELEBRATE!

THEME: Celebrating

The words "party time!" instantly grab the attention of socially eager kids. Often, though, the party scene in a teenager's world is anything but a positive experience. For example, a Search Institute study of sixth- to 12th-graders found that 31 percent frequently attend parties where peers drink. Sixty-one percent of seniors say they frequently attend such parties.

As a result, some kids may think non-Christians "have all the fun." Yet the Bible is filled with positive reasons to "party"—to celebrate. This meeting challenges your kids to look for healthy reasons and ways to celebrate in day-to-day living and on special occasions.

 Before the Meeting

Decorate the room with balloons and streamers. Write each letter in the word "C-E-L-E-B-R-A-T-E" on a separate sheet of colorful paper. If you expect more than nine people, make multiple copies so each person has at least one letter. Gather art supplies, balloons, markers, and newsprint or a chalkboard. Make sure everyone has a copy of *The Youth Bible*.

▶ 1. What's Happening?

As they arrive, give kids each at least one letter from the word "C-E-L-E-B-R-A-T-E." Without explaining what the word is, have the group work together to discover and spell out the meeting topic. If you have more than one set of letters, mention how many sets there are.

When the group discovers the solution, have everyone cheer, tear up the letters in small pieces and throw them in the air like confetti.

When the commotion dies down, ask: **How did it feel to celebrate discovering the meeting theme? When have you had similar feelings of joy and celebration? Some people say Christians don't have much fun. Do you agree or disagree? Why?**

Say: **Our faith isn't a dreary faith; it's a faith that celebrates God's goodness. Let's look at celebrations in the Bible to learn how to celebrate in Christ-like ways today.**

▶ 2. Biblical Celebrations

Form groups of three or more and assign each group one of the following passages in *The Youth Bible*: Psalm 81:1-10; Isaiah 40:1-11; Jeremiah 31:1-17; Mark 2:18-22; or John 21:1-14. (You don't have to use all the passages.)

Say: **Look for why and how celebration occurs in your passage. Present to the rest of the group, in a joyful way, the key ideas you discover. Choose from these celebration ideas: prepare a choral reading or a rap, write new words to a familiar song or hymn, make up a skit or make a banner.**

Point out the art supplies and give groups time to prepare. Have each group present its celebration activity.

Then ask: **What's the difference between a celebration and a party? How can there be celebration during grief or despair? How is hope a part of celebration? Based on your Bible study, what are some reasons to celebrate?**

Write ideas on a chalkboard or on newsprint.

▶ 3. Celebrate Now

Have volunteers read aloud these devotions in *The Youth Bible*: "Remembering Matt" (p. 725) and "Party Blues" (p. 967). Discuss the questions that follow each story.

Ask: **What emotions are involved in these stories? Why was there a reason to celebrate?**

Give kids each an inflated balloon and a marker and have them write on the balloon as many different types of teenage celebrations as they can think of. Have people tell the group what they wrote.

Ask: **Which celebrations are most impor-** tant? least important? How can these celebrations be both happy and sad?

▶ 4. Day-to-Day Celebrations

Ask: **What daily events do you celebrate? How do these small, daily celebrations keep you going? How can you celebrate God in your daily life?**

Select a story from these devotions in *The Youth Bible*: "Shout Out Loud!" (p. 530), "Ha!" (p. 655) or "A Dark Victory" (p. 1096). Ask someone to read the story aloud. Then discuss the questions.

Ask: **How did the people in this story celebrate the day-to-day events in life?**

Encourage kids to look for opportunities to celebrate in the next few days. Brainstorm small ways to celebrate the daily events. For example, celebrate finishing a term paper by riding bikes with friends. List on newsprint the ideas kids come up with.

▶ 5. Plan a Celebration

Have kids look through the celebration ideas under "Consider ... " in *The Youth Bible* devotions on celebrating. As a group, choose one celebration idea to put into action. Assign kids different responsibilities in the celebration.

Close by standing in a circle and singing a song of celebration, such as "I Saw the Light," "Victory Chant" or "I Will Celebrate" from *The Group Songbook* (Group Books).

BODY LIFE

THEME: Church

It's easy for idealistic teenagers to become cynical when they look at the church. Quick to cite human flaws and wavering values, Christian teenagers sometimes struggle to keep their enthusiasm for church from turning to disillusionment. This meeting will challenge your kids to channel their enthusiasm into positive action on behalf of the church.

▶ Before the Meeting

Make one photocopy of the "Battle Plan" handout for every two people. Gather newsprint, markers, pencils and a copy of *The Youth Bible* for each student.

▶ 1. The Human Machine

Say: **We're going to start our meeting by building a human machine. We'll begin with one person who'll make up a sound and a movement. One by one the rest of you will attach to an existing part, adding your own sound and movement. Your movement will need to depend on the movements already established by other people in the machine. You can build on different levels by using a chair or lying on the floor.**

Choose your best risk-taker to be the base to which the next person will attach. Have kids each keep up their particular sounds and move-

ments until all the kids are joined and the machine is complete.

Say: **Our production is way down. I'm afraid we'll have to speed things up a bit.** Have kids go faster. Increase the speed as much as you think is safe!

Then say: **Okay. We made it! You can slow back to normal. Oops! Looks like it's vacation time. We need to slow down to just a bare minimum.** Have kids see how slow they can go without stopping.

Say: **Great! Come back to normal now. It's just a plain old day at the machine. But wait . . . something's happening!** Pull out one kid who's in a vital spot where several others are attached. Kids should allow the machine to slowly fall apart. If they don't get the idea on their own, then give some physical clues to show that's what should happen.

As your machine is lying in pieces on the floor, ask: **How did you feel when one person pulled out of our machine? How is** this machine like our church? How is each part of a machine like people who are part of the church?

Say: **For a church to run smoothly, all the people involved need to do their part at the same speed and with the same purpose as everyone else. We're going to take a look at the good things that can happen when church members work together, and some of the painful things that happen when they don't.**

▶ 2. Show Me!

Form five groups. Assign each group one of the following devotions and passages from *The Youth Bible*: "The Place to Belong," Acts 2:36-47; "Watching Every Detail," 1 Corinthians 12:12-27; "Friends or Foes?" Ephesians 4:1-6; "Sticking Together," Philippians 2:1-11; "Family of Friends," Hebrews 10:19-39.

Say: **Read through the devotion, scripture, and questions together. Then come up with a one-word theme for what you've read. Plan a pantomime to illustrate that theme for the whole group.**

Allow a few minutes for groups to study and plan. Then pull everyone together and have groups each perform their pantomime. If the other kids have trouble guessing the theme, have the performers explain it. (Given in the same order as above, suggested themes are: belonging, body, unity, support and commitment.) List the key point for each pantomime on a large sheet of newsprint.

Say: **The passages we've studied show us these five things God has in mind for a healthy church. How would knowing about these five points have helped our human machine? Which of these points do you think is the most important? How does our youth group show these characteristics?**

▶ 3. Church Blueprint

Ask for a volunteer to draw the outline of a body on a large sheet of newsprint.

Say: **We're going to put together a diagram of a healthy church, using this body as a model. As we work up our diagram, keep in mind the five characteristics of a healthy church we discovered in our Bible study.**

Encourage kids to draw and label parts of the body to explain how the church works together. For example, the pastor might be part of the head and the mouth, because he does a lot of the speaking. Members who help each other could be the hands. Those who pray and encourage could be the heart.

Ask: **How does our church compare to this body diagram? How does our youth group compare? Where would you like to see our diagram made stronger?**

▶ 4. Battle Plan

Say: **We want to come up with a battle plan to make our church and our youth group more like the healthy body we just drew.**

Have kids pair off. Give a photocopy of the handout "Battle Plan" and a pencil to each pair. Allow three or four minutes for kids to come up with a few ideas for each section. Then have pairs share their ideas with the rest of the group. Compile a list of ideas that are "greatest hits" on newsprint or a chalkboard.

Say: **Each of us is connected to the others in the church. You're already an important part of the body of Christ. Hearing the great ideas you've come up with makes me really excited about the future of our group and our church!**

To close, hold hands and sing "Lord, Be Glorified" from *The Group Songbook* (Group Books).

BATTLE PLAN

NEW RECRUITS—What's the best plan for handling visitors who come to youth group or church?

BEHIND-THE-LINES SUPPORT—What are your interests and talents? List them. How can you plug them into the youth group or church?

CASUALTY REPORT—Do you know people in the church or youth group who are hurting? What can you do to show support for them?

GOOD CONDUCT MEDAL—Who works to keep your youth group/church unified? What kind of award can you design to honor them?

DOING OUR PART

THEME: Creation

God gave us a wonderful world to live in. We benefit from its resources, but with the privileges also comes responsibility. This meeting will help your kids see the wonder of God's creation, how he wants us to care for it, and what we can do to make sure our world will still be liveable and enjoyable 50 years from now.

Before the Meeting

Cut 3×5 cards into three sections to make a business-size card for each kid. Gather uncooked eggs, markers, two large bowls, a world map or globe, paper and pencils.

1. Creations Eggstraordinaire

Give kids each an uncooked egg, and distribute markers. Explain that kids are to transform their eggs into globes by using markers to carefully draw the earth's continental shapes and seas on them. You might want to have a globe or a world map available for a visual reference.

Give kids several minutes to complete their creations, then ask: **How did it feel creating the world? How was this like and unlike God creating the world in the first place? Was it easy to get everything in place where it belonged? How do you think God might've felt while creating our earth?**

Carefully gather the "globe-eggs" in a bowl and set them aside.

2. Our Wonderland World

Ask: **What's special about God's creation?**

After kids answer, have them turn to p. 574 in *The Youth Bible* and read "Moment of Wonder." Then read Proverbs 8:22-31 together and discuss the questions from the devotion.

3. Eggcological Disaster

Without telling kids what's going on, get out another bowl and begin cracking their globe-eggs into it. After you empty the contents of each egg, crush the shell. Kids will likely protest, but don't give any explanation.

After all the egg shells have been crushed, ask: **How did it feel when I began breaking and crushing your eggs? How might that be like how God feels when we don't take proper care of what he created for us?**

How does that affect the way you look at caring for God's creation?

 4. Earth Users Guide

Say: **Let's take a look at how God wants us to treat his creation.** Form groups of about four and have them each read the following two devotions from *The Youth Bible:* "Will We Ever Learn?" (p. 4) and "Trashed Out" (p. 839).

Give groups a few minutes to read the devotions and passages. Then give these instructions: **We're going to help God out. Based on these passages, write a users guide to go along with planet Earth. You'll have to keep it short, but try to cover the main points you think the Creator would want the users of this product to remember.**

Distribute paper and pencils. Give groups about 10 minutes to create their users guides, then have them each report on what they wrote.

 5. Creation Reminders

After groups report, brainstorm a list of ways teenagers can follow the users guide to care for the planet God's given us. Have them look at the "Consider . . ." sections of the devotions they've used for ideas. They might list such things as recycling soft drink cans, planting new trees, or conserving use of gasoline.

When you've brainstormed at least 10 ideas, give kids each a blank business-size card. Say: **Take a look at the list of ideas we've brainstormed and choose two you'll concentrate on following. Write one idea on each side of your card. Keep it in your wallet or purse to remind you to work at caring for God's creation.**

Form a circle and let kids pray sentence prayers, thanking God for our wonderful world or asking for help in caring for the earth.

 6. The Big Scramble

Wrap up your session by creating a fun snack with the eggs. You might make omelets, scrambled eggs, french toast, dutch pancakes, jelly-filled crepes or custard pies. If you don't use the eggs for a snack, be sure to take them home in a covered container and use them—throwing them away wouldn't fit too well with this session!

NAME THAT CULT

THEME: Cults

Cults can attract anyone. They give people a strong sense of purpose and belonging—something we all desperately need but can't always find.

Unfortunately, cults are almost always deceptive. The truth about life, even God, is compromised as cult leaders manipulate facts and feelings in order to gain control over people's lives. This meeting focuses on helping kids learn to recognize and respond to cults.

quickly lose their attraction once you find out what they're really like.

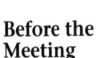

Before the Meeting

Gather several recent newspapers, posterboard, markers and 3×5 cards. Make sure everyone has a copy of *The Youth Bible*.

1. The Fine Print

Distribute portions of recent newspapers (not the want ads) as kids arrive. Explain that kids are to look for ads that look great at first but lose their appeal once you read the "fine print." Have kids share the examples they find with the rest of the group.

Ask: **Which ads did you like at first? How did you feel after you read the fine print? How might these ads be compared to cults?**

Say: **It's good to read the fine print in advertising, so you can know exactly what you're getting into. Cults are like that too. They may look good at first, but they**

2. Draw Your Conclusions

Form five groups (a group may be one person). Assign each group one of the following devotions and passages from *The Youth Bible*: "Deadly Deception," Matthew 7:15-29; "Good News, Bad News," Galatians 1:1-10; "Hazardous to Your Health," Ephesians 4:11-16; "Fatal Attraction," Colossians 2:1-15; "Christian Frauds," 2 John 7-11.

Say: **From the information you gather in your reading, I want each group to think up a warning about cults that can be made into a poster.**

Distribute posterboard and markers. When groups have created their posters, give them each an opportunity to explain their posters to the others. Congratulate kids on their creativity and have them put the posters up on the walls.

Ask: **Are there any other warnings about cults your group came up with besides these? Of all the warnings we've mentioned, which are the most important? Explain.**

Say: **Typically, cults use deception to lure people, then manipulate their emotions to keep them trapped. But just a little research will help you discover a cult's true methods and motives.**

▶ 3. Truth or Fiction

Give kids each a 3×5 card and a marker. Have them write "Truth" on one side of the card and "Fiction" on the other.

Say: **Most people think they could never be fooled into becoming part of a cult. But it happens more easily than you'd think. Most cults have some good things to say, and they can sound pretty convincing. Let's find out just how easy it is to be taken in by things that sound true but really aren't. I want each of you to think of something to say about yourself. It can be truth or fiction, but your goal is to try to make it sound as believable as possible.**

Form a circle and have kids each tell their truth or fiction. After each statement, have the rest of the group display either the truth or fiction side of their cards to indicate whether they believe the statement is true or false. After all the cards are raised, have the person tell whether the statement actually was true. Continue until everyone has given at least one statement about themselves.

Then ask: **How did it feel to try to guess whether people were telling the truth? What clues did you use to tell whether others were telling the truth about themselves? What clues could you use to tell whether a group is really a cult?**

Say: **One thing that might help you uncover a group's true nature is to read what people who aren't in the group say about it. Let's look at some other ways you can protect yourself from cults.**

▶ 4. Take Action!

Have kids each find a partner. Explain that each pair is to come up with one thing they can do to protect themselves from being taken in by a cult. Have pairs share their ideas with the rest of the group.

Encourage kids to learn more about cults on their own, especially cults their friends may be involved in.

Say: **Jesus said, "You will know the truth. And the truth will make you free." Let's close by affirming to each other that knowing the truth about cults will set us free from the chance of falling into one.**

Have kids turn to each other and say, "The truth will make you free."

NEVER WITHOUT HOPE

THEME: Death

People who watch over dying loved ones often cling to the thought: Where there's life, there's hope. Amazingly, Christians find hope even in death. This meeting will help your kids explore their feelings about death and develop a healthy Christian perspective on this important and frequently avoided topic.

▶ Before the Meeting

Bring enough newspaper obituary pages for each student to have at least one. Gather slips of paper, an old hat, several paper grocery bags, a squirt bottle, paper and pencils. Make sure everyone has a copy of *The Youth Bible*.

▶ 1. Out of the Picture

As kids arrive, have them write their names on slips of paper and drop the paper into a hat. Ask someone in your group to pick a number between one and five. Draw that number of names out of the hat. Act very solemn as you read the names.

Say: **I'm sorry to tell you that these people are now officially "dead" to our group. They may not speak or interact with us in any way.**

Quietly place a paper grocery bag over the head of each of the kids who "died." If kids react with giggling, stress the fact that you'd appreciate their cooperation in keeping this a serious activity.

Then ask the others: **How is this like or unlike the way death comes to people? How would our lives be different without these members of our group? How would we feel if they were really dead?**

Say: **Now it's time to revive our friends. You guys help me pull off those bags.** As the bags come off, give the emerging kids a shot of water with the squirt bottle to "revive" them.

Ask them: **How did it feel to be dead for a few minutes? How has this activity affected your feelings about death?**

Choose one or two of the following devotions from *The Youth Bible* to read aloud: "He's Gone" (p. 192); "Bittersweet" (p. 641); "Goodbye to a Pigtail-Puller" (p. 1093). Discuss the questions at the end.

Then ask: **What's the scariest thing about**

death for you? Do you feel good or bad about getting these feelings out into the open? Explain.

 2. Giving Support

Read aloud the devotion "Sharing Sadness" (p. 1076 in *The Youth Bible*).

Ask: **Why is the support of others so important when people are grieving?**

Give kids each a page of obituaries from the newspaper.

Say: **Find and circle one obituary for this activity.**

Then ask: **Why did you circle the person you circled? Did his or her name, situation, age or circumstances attract you? Do you know this person? How does this person's death affect you?**

Take a moment to pray for the family and friends who've experienced this loved one's death.

 3. A Closer Death

Ask: **Who'd be willing to tell about a death that's touched you personally? How did you react to it? How did God help you through it? In what ways is the death easier to live with now? Harder?** Encourage kids to be sensitive to each other's feelings as they share.

Pass out paper and pencils. Have kids turn to 2 Samuel 1:17-27 in *The Youth Bible*. Explain David's relationship to Saul and Jonathan. Then read aloud the passage and the accompanying devotion, "A Tribute."

Then say: **David chose to write a song in response to the loss of two people who were important to him. What would you do to express your feelings about the loss of a friend or family member? Would you write a song? a poem? draw a picture?**

Give kids a few minutes to work on their tributes. Then invite volunteers to share what they've written or drawn.

Ask: **How does remembering help? Why is it hard?**

 4. If You Knew

Have a volunteer read aloud "Loving Memories" (p. 992 in *The Youth Bible*).

Ask: **Do you think it would be easier to face your own death or face the death of someone you love? Explain.**

Have someone read aloud Mark 14:12-26. Then ask: **What were Jesus' priorities before his own death? Do you think people have an appointed time to die? Explain.**

 5. Affirm the Hope

Break into three groups. Assign each group one of the following passages: Isaiah 25:6-9; John 14:1-3; and 1 Corinthians 15:50-55. Have groups each report on what their passage teaches about life after death.

Ask: **How do these assurances of life after death affect your own feelings about death? What hope do you find in these verses?**

Invite kids to put this hope into their own words. Let these phrases of hope be your closing prayer.

YOU CALL IT

THEME: Decision Making

Kids often wait for a retreat or a youth conference to make decisions about following God. What they fail to see is that it's daily decisions that make or break their walk with God. This meeting challenges kids to demonstrate their loyalty to God by making good decisions about their lives every day.

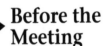

Before the Meeting

Gather 3×5 cards, markers, paper, pencils, tape, and newsprint. Make sure everyone has a copy of *The Youth Bible*.

1. Choices Unseen

Form two teams and give each team a stack of 3×5 cards and a marker.

Say: **Think of all the decisions you have to make in life and write each one on a separate 3×5 card. Your decisions can be big, such as who to date or where to go to college, but also include everyday decisions, such as how to pass geometry or whether to go to a party with friends. As you write your decisions, lay your cards on the floor end to end. Your goal is to make your line of cards longer than the other team's. You have three minutes. Go!**

When time is up, congratulate the winning team and have kids read aloud several of the decisions they listed.

After each one is read, ask: **How would you go about making a decision like this?**

After you've discussed several samples, ask: **How are our decisions a way to show loyalty to God?**

2. How Not to Do It

Have kids sit in a circle. Read aloud "Living With Deadlines" (p. 187 in *The Youth Bible*).

Ask: **What do you think about Wayne's decision-making method? How would you have dealt with his situation differently?**

Say: **We all have our own ways of making decisions, but even the best decision-makers blow it sometimes.**

Ask volunteers to tell crazy ways people make decisions; for example, flipping a coin, reading their horoscopes, or consulting a psychic. Kids may laugh at their responses, but be aware that many of your kids may have made decisions using one of these methods.

Say: **Making decisions can be scary, and it's easy to fall into false methods to make the task easier. Now let's work together to see how we can make wise choices— choices that demonstrate our faith in God.**

▶ 3. You Can Do It

Have a volunteer read aloud Deuteronomy 30:11-20.

Ask: **In this passage, what choice did God offer? How is this choice like ones we make every day?**

Say: **Every choice we make can bring us nearer to God or pull us further away from him.**

Remind kids of Wayne's story.

Ask: **Which direction did Wayne's choice lead?**

Distribute paper and pencils. Lead kids in the second "Consider . . ." idea (p. 187). When everyone is finished, have kids share their discoveries.

Ask kids to form groups of three. Assign each group one or two of the following devotions and passages from *The Youth Bible*: "To Fly or Not," Job 28:20-28; "Always Be Ready," Matthew 25:1-13; "A Soldier Decides," Luke 9:51-62; "But I Didn't Think . . . ," Luke 16:19-31; "Different Strokes for Different Folks," Romans 14:5-12; or "Who's Gonna Know?" Ephesians 5:6-20. (You don't have to use all the devotions and passages.)

As kids read, have them look for actions and attitudes that lead to godly choices. Then bring everyone together and have groups share their discoveries. Record kids' responses on a sheet of newsprint.

▶ 4. Easier Said Than Done

Ask: **Even when we know how to make wise choices, we still don't always make choices that please God. Why do you think that is?**

Say: **Let's create a personal-decision profile quiz to help us see what kind of decision-makers we are.**

Have kids help you choose six of the decision-making ideas and attitudes you listed on newsprint as the basis for the quiz. Number the six ideas. Give kids each a sheet of paper and a pencil.

Say: **Number your papers one to six. For each of these ideas, write "A" if you always make decisions this way, "M" if you do most of the time, "S" if you do sometimes, and "N" if you never do.**

When kids are finished, say: **Give yourself 6 points for each A, 4 points for each M, 2 points for each S and 0 points for each N.**

Give kids a minute to score themselves, then have them total their points. Read aloud the following suggested rankings to help kids see how well they make decisions:

0 to 9—You let other people make your decisions for you.

10 to 19—You care more about appearances than what is best for you.

20 to 29—You have the courage to seek God's best in most circumstances.

30 to 36—Congratulations! You know how to walk in a way that pleases God!

▶ 5. Decisive Changes

Form a circle. Have kids close their eyes and think about the quiz they just took. Encourage kids each to choose one good decision-making method they'll begin to use, and to tell God about their choice.

After a few moments of silence, close with prayer, thanking God for giving us ways to make decisions that are wise and pleasing to him.

DOWN, BUT NOT OUT

THEME: Depression

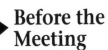

Before the Meeting

Photocopy the "Blues Busters" handout. Gather paper slips, pencils, balloons, darts, newsprint, markers and a cheery greeting card. Make sure there is a copy of *The Youth Bible* for each group member.

1. Burst Bubbles

Distribute slips of paper and pencils. Have kids each write on their slip one true-to-life problem that teenagers face, beginning with "You have just ..." For example, You have just flunked a math test after studying for it for over three hours.

When kids finish writing, have them fold their slips and put them in a pile. Let the "windier" kids in the group blow up one balloon for each slip, while the others randomly attach the slips to a bulletin board. Then attach the balloons to the bulletin board so that each balloon covers

Life for a Christian should be full of joy, right? But Christians of all ages deal with real problems, including depression. Depression can hit hard during adolescence, when kids experience lots of biological change and emotional upheaval. Christian kids need to know that Jesus Christ can offer real comfort when they feel down.

one slip.

Have kids take turns throwing darts at the board. (Carefully monitor this process!) When kids pop a balloon, they'll read their slip aloud, tell how they would feel if the problem happened to them, and what they would do about it.

Say: **Life is filled with problems—it can get downright depressing, even for a Christian. Let's see what kind of hope God offers when we feel down.**

2. Is There Any Hope?

Form three groups. Assign each group one of the following devotions and passages from *The Youth Bible*: "Stirring Up Life," Job 7:1-8; "The Wall Came Tumbling Down," Psalm 30; or "Positive," Isaiah 35. Give groups about five minutes to read through the devotion and passage, discuss the questions, and come up with at least one thing from the devotion or passage that shows how God provides hope.

Bring everyone together and have groups share their stories and report on their findings.

Say: **God offers hope. Sometimes *we* can be the hope he offers to others.**

3. Busting the Blues

Distribute the "Blues Busters" handouts. Give kids a few minutes to complete it. Then discuss the responses as a class and compile a tally on newsprint to see if there are clear leaders in any of the blues busters categories.

Ask: **What's the first action you take when you want to do something about feeling down? What do you normally do when you see a friend who's down? In your opinion, what is the best "cure" for depression?** (You may wish to point out here that forms of serious, clinical depression are best treated with professional counseling and, in some cases, medication. Give kids some information about the availability of such help, and be sure they know you're available to discuss their needs in this area.)

Say: **It can be fun to offer God's hope to someone who needs it. And if you're feeling down yourself, sometimes a good way to feel better is to reach out to someone else.**

4. Card Campaign

Show kids the greeting card you brought. Ask them to think of a person most of them know who's going through tough times. (If more than one name is offered, help the kids decide who needs the encouragement most.)

Say: **This card is the beginning of our card campaign. We'll send it to (name) to show our support and to offer God's hope.**

Pass the card around and have kids sign it individually.

Ask: **How do you think (name) will feel when (he or she) receives our card? Why is it so encouraging to get a cheerful note from someone?**

Take an offering for cards. You might have kids elect a leader to be in charge of keeping the card campaign going. The leader would keep cards and stamps on hand and remind kids to bring up the names of people who could use a dose of encouragement and support from the youth group.

Have kids stand in a circle and hold hands. Pray sentence prayers asking God to give them hope, or to help them know how to offer hope to a friend this week.

BLUES BUSTERS

Directions: Complete the sentences below with the first thought that comes into your mind.

1. These things make me depressed:

2. One thing that usually gets me into a better mood is:

3. These are the people I feel safe talking to about things that depress me:

4. If I saw a friend having a "down day," I would
   - suggest we go to this movie:

   - take over this food:

   - have him or her listen to this song:

   - suggest we do this activity:

   - suggest we go to this place:

CHIN UP!

THEME: Discouragement

Discouragement is nothing new to teenagers—they experience it on a regular basis. Kids run into setbacks in almost every area of life as they discover and test their abilities at home, school, church and in relationships. Use this meeting to help teenagers learn that God's power can turn the most discouraging situations into positive ones.

▶ **Before the Meeting**

Gather large sheets of newsprint, markers, paper and pencils. Make sure everyone has a copy of *The Youth Bible*.

▶ **1. Barometers**

Have kids stand with their hands reaching high over their heads. Tell them to use their bodies as barometers of how someone would feel if certain things happened. For example, kids might shrink or slowly bend over with each event.

Read the list of failures from "Failure Turned Around" (p. 598 in *The Youth Bible*). Then read the hope breakers from "Hope Breakers and Makers" (p. 1321 in *The Youth Bible*).

Ask: **How did you feel during this activity? How is this like or unlike the way you feel** when you're discouraged? Of all the things I mentioned, **which would be the most discouraging to you?**

▶ **2. Down, but Not Out**

Say: **Today's session is about discouragement. We're going to look at reasons to keep a positive attitude, even when things aren't going the way we want.**

Form three groups. Give groups each a marker and a large sheet of newsprint. Assign each group one of the following devotions and passages in *The Youth Bible*: "49,999 … and Counting," Genesis 15:1-6; "Specially Chosen," Numbers 21:4-9; and "Failure Turned Around," Ecclesiastes 1:2-11.

When groups have read the stories and scripture passages, say: **I want you to draw something on your sheet of paper that** symbolizes the struggle with discouragement and the ultimate victory experienced by the character in your story.

Then bring everyone together, and have groups share their symbols and stories.

Ask: **How do you feel about the people in these stories? What gave them the courage to keep going in the face of discouraging circumstances? How could their examples affect your life?**

 3. I'm So Down

Form two groups. Have kids choose one person in their group to be the "counselee." Assign each group one of the following devotions from *The Youth Bible*: "Is There Hope?" (p. 875) or "Always Be Ready" (p. 953). Have groups each read their devotion, passage, and the scriptures from the "For More, See ..." section.

Have the counselees each role play their character's discouragement as the rest of the group counsels them with the principles gleaned from scripture.

 4. A Second Chance

Ask a volunteer to read aloud the story "God Is Here" (p. 794 in *The Youth Bible*). Lead kids in discussing the questions that follow the story.

Ask: **Do you think Todd had good reason to feel hopeless about his relationship with Erin? Explain. How did God's presence in the situation make a difference? How has God helped in a "hopeless" situation in your life?**

 5. Be Encouraged

Give kids each paper and pencils. Lead them in the first "Consider ..." activity in "Always Be Ready" (p. 953 in *The Youth Bible*).

Say: **Keep your list in your Bible and read over it the next time you're feeling discouraged.**

Close in prayer, thanking God for encouraging us when we're discouraged.

THOSE DUBIOUS DOUBTS

THEME: Doubt

Everyone doubts sometimes. When the future looks bleak or the world seems against you, it's easy to question the things that hold your life together. Even the Bible "heroes of the faith" struggled with trusting God's word. But doubting can become a threat to our health as Christians when it paralyzes our obedience or causes us to give up on finding the truth.

This meeting will help kids explore their own doubts and find ways to continue in faith, even when doubt creeps in.

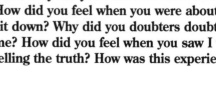

▶ Before the Meeting

You'll need 11 thoroughly hard-boiled eggs and one unboiled egg, all set in an egg carton. Set up 11 chairs in a row, facing an open area. Have sections of a newspaper to hand out. Also gather newsprint, tape, pencils and paper. Make sure everyone has a copy of *The Youth Bible*.

▶ 1. A Doubtful Eggsample

Tell kids you're going to test their doubt levels with a potentially messy challenge.

Hold up the carton of eggs and say: **These are all hard-boiled eggs. Do you believe me? Well, some of you look doubtful, so I'll prove it.**

Take the one unboiled egg, hold it over a wastebasket and squeeze.

When the egg bursts, say: **Okay, so I must have forgotten to boil one of them. But the** rest are definitely boiled. **How many of you believe me?**

Invite some or all of the kids who said they believed you to stand in front of one of the chairs. Hand kids two sections of newspaper: one to cover the chair and one to use as a shield. Then set an egg on each chair.

Say: **Since you said you believe me, I'm giving you the chance to prove that you have no doubts at all about the fact that these eggs are hard-boiled.**

Then say: **On "go," I want you to fall back into the chair behind you. Go!**

Have the volunteers stand up to show that you were indeed telling the truth. If you wish, salvage the squashed eggs by having kids help you make egg salad at the close of the meeting.

Ask: **Why did you believers believe me? How did you feel when you were about to sit down? Why did you doubters doubt me? How did you feel when you saw I was telling the truth? How was this experience** like doubting God? How was it different? What is the toughest thing about having doubts?

 2. Bible Doubters

Form five groups (a group can be one person) and assign each group one of these passages: Genesis 17:15-19; Judges 6:33-40; Psalm 13; Isaiah 7:10-16; or John 20:19-31. While kids are reading their passages, tape a sheet of newsprint to the wall and write on it these four questions:

● What was the promise or event that God wanted the Bible character(s) to believe in?

● How is it evident that the character(s) was doubting?

● What did the character(s) do to try to overcome the doubt?

● How did God respond to the doubter in this case?

Give groups each a sheet of paper and a pencil and have them work together to write answers to your four questions. When everyone is finished, have them share the biblical situation and their answers.

Ask: **In what cases did God intervene in the situation with supernatural events? Can we expect such actions from God today? In what other ways can we experience assurance from God? In what ways can Christian friends help us when we're doubting?**

Say: **Let's see how someone like you dealt with doubt.**

 3. Act on the Spot

Use the "Riding Out the Storm" story (p. 1083 in *The Youth Bible*) to get kids thinking about practical applications of the scriptures they've

studied. Tell kids that as you read the story aloud, you'll pause before certain phrases, point to someone and say "Ding!" This will alert that person to act out the phrase you're about to read. Encourage kids to be creative. After each impromptu act, continue with the story.

Here are the phrases kids will act out: "youngest person in history"; "like a drug to him"; "violent storm almost capsized his little sloop"; "barely survived the waterspout"; "almost went crazy with despair and doubt"; "snapped to his senses and doused the fire"; "cheering crowds, honking cars, and blasting steam whistles"; "wrestled two great enemies."

After the reading, ask: **How were Robin's doubts like those of the Bible characters? What doubts do you have that remind you of Robin or the Bible characters? How can you deal with your doubts?**

▶ 4. This One Thing

Have kids move to the "Consider . . ." section of the same devotion (p. 1083 in *The Youth Bible*). Give kids each pencil and paper and have them complete the statement "The one thing I doubt the most is . . . " Have kids pair up and share their doubt with their partner. Partners will then give encouragement to deal with the doubt.

Bring the group back together. Ask kids each to share their partner's doubt and the encouragement they gave. Have the whole group brainstorm further ways of dealing with the doubt. Encourage kids to recall God's promises and specific scriptures that apply to each doubt.

Close the meeting with prayer, thanking God for his patience with us when we're doubting and for the help and hope we get in scripture and from our Christian friends.

CHOOSE NOT TO ABUSE

THEME: Drugs and Alcohol

Statistics show that approximately one-third of teenagers try alcohol by their freshman year in high school. This in turn may lead to drug abuse, as 61 percent of drug abusers admit the first drug they used was alcohol. This session helps your kids explore biblical reasons to choose not to abuse.

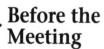
Before the Meeting

You'll need a bicycle, a stopwatch and cones or chairs to set up an obstacle course in a parking lot or large open area of the church building. Gather newsprint, markers, two boxes, a package of cookies, a bottle of hydrogen peroxide and about a month's worth of recent newspapers. Make sure everyone has a copy of *The Youth Bible*.

▶ 1. It's a Maze

Have kids help you set up an obstacle course using chairs or cones. Time kids as they go through the course on a bicycle. Set up a time sheet on a large sheet of newsprint and have kids record their own score.

After everyone has competed, have kids repeat the course—this time with the handicap of using only one leg. Have kids post their new scores next to their previous scores.

Ask: **How did you feel about competing the first time through the course? the second time? In real life, would you purposely give your body or mind a handicap?**

Say: **Millions of kids intentionally impair their minds and bodies every day with drugs and alcohol. Today we're going to talk about some kids who found out the hard way how easy it is to get involved in substance abuse.**

▶ 2. Impaired!

Form four groups. Assign each group one of the following devotions and passages from *The Youth Bible*: "Under the Influence," Esther 1:4-12; "Not Alone ...," Romans 7:14-25; "The Lost Weekend," Romans 13:11-14; and "Serving Something," 1 Corinthians 6:12-20. Have groups each discuss the questions at the end of their devotion. Explain that each group is to choose a person to play the part of the main character in

57

their devotion. These people will each say, "I am an alcoholic" and briefly relate their story to the entire group (as in an Alcoholics Anonymous meeting).

When groups are ready, bring everyone together for the presentations. After each character has spoken, let the rest of the kids offer advice on how to deal with the problem in light of the passages they've just read.

Ask: **Why did these people choose to abuse alcohol and drugs? What excuses do these people commonly make to themselves? How can kids avoid the addiction trap?**

▶ 3. Making a Choice

Before the meeting, place two boxes upside down on a table. Label one "A" and the other "B." Place enough cookies under box A for each person to have a few. Place a bottle of hydrogen peroxide under box B.

Tell kids to choose either box A or B for today's snack. Explain that what's in one box is good, and what's in the other box could have serious consequences.

Invite kids to gather by the box they choose. Then reveal the contents of the boxes.

Before sharing the cookies with everyone, ask: **How did you feel when you had to make a choice? How was that choice like deciding whether or not to use drugs and alcohol? How were the consequences different from the consequences in real life?**

Pass the plate of cookies around the class and assure kids that you're not really going to let anyone drink hydrogen peroxide.

▶ 4. Paying the Price

Put a large stack of recent newspapers on a table and lead kids in the second "Consider ..." activity from the devotion "Under the Influence." Have kids gather articles about drunk-driving accidents. After several minutes, gather everyone and have kids share the articles they found.

Ask: **How do these stories make you feel? What's an appropriate way for us to respond to these tragedies?**

Lead in a time of prayer for the victims and their families, praying that those who are driving drunk will stop before others are hurt.

▶ 5. Support Huddle

Say: **These devotions and newspaper articles have shown us what can happen when we choose to abuse. Each of you may know people whose lives were ruined by their choice to use drugs or alcohol. But I doubt that any of you can think of people whose lives were ruined because they chose not to abuse. I hope you'll make the right choice.**

Close by forming a "hug huddle" with kids' arms around each other. Pray for God to keep kids strong in their commitments to keep their bodies pure and free from drugs and alcohol.

FOREVER

THEME: Eternal Life

It's hard to imagine forever. But the promise of life forever is central to the message of the gospel. Many kids (and adults) are a little foggy about the glorious future God promises for believers. Use this meeting to help your kids understand God's gift of eternal life.

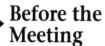

Before the Meeting

Gather six square pieces of light-color posterboard, markers, tape, ribbon, balloons and a copy of *The Youth Bible* for each person.

▶ 1. Never-Ending Joy

Have kids form two groups. Ask each group to brainstorm at least five things they wish would never end (a chocolate malt or a vacation in Hawaii, for example).

Bring the groups together and have them share their ideas.

Say: **These things sound great to me. Now we're going to talk about something that's even better!**

Direct kids to the devotion "A Bit of Heaven" (p. 1349 in *The Youth Bible*). Have a volunteer read it aloud.

Then ask: **What does the word "heaven" bring to mind? How does thinking about** eternal life make you feel?

Say: **We all have ideas about what eternal life in heaven is like. One** thing we know is that it is God's gift to us, through Jesus' sacrifice. Let's take a closer look at the gift.

▶ 2. The Gift

Form five groups. (A group can be as small as one person.) Assign each group one of the following devotions from *The Youth Bible*: "Safe Under the Falls," Isaiah 12; "Going the Distance," Daniel 12:1-3; "Good Enough," Luke 13:22-30; "The Ultimate Price," John 3:1-21; and "We Will All Be Changed," 1 Corinthians 15:35-58.

Have groups read their devotions and related scripture passages, then discuss the questions at the end.

Give each group a posterboard square and a marker. Say: **I want you to come up with a** one-sentence summary of what you learned about eternal life from your devotion and passage. Write the sentence on your cardboard square.

As groups are working, write "God's Gift: Eternal Life" on the remaining posterboard square. When kids have finished, bring everyone together and have groups share their one-sentence summaries.

Ask a representative from each group to bring the posterboard squares to the front. Add your square to the other five, and have kids help you tape the squares together to form a box. Have a volunteer tie a ribbon around the box.

Ask: **How is eternal life like a gift? What do you like best about this gift? What's the neatest earthly gift you ever received? How did you respond to the giver? How does the gift of eternal life compare with that gift? How can you share the gift of eternal life with others?**

▶ 3. Bright and Beautiful

Have kids close their eyes and listen as you read aloud the description of heaven in Revelation 22:1-5. Then distribute balloons and markers.

Say: **Blow up your balloon and write on it the thing you're most anticipating about the eternal future God has planned for his people.**

Have kids each share what they wrote, then tape their balloon to a ceiling light.

When all the balloons have been taped so that the light shines through them, ask: **How is our balloon display like your idea of heaven? How is it different? How have your ideas about eternal life changed as our meeting has progressed?**

▶ 4. Saying Thanks

Say: **It's important to remember that this gift of eternal life didn't come cheaply. Gaining eternal life for us was the main purpose behind Jesus' life, ministry, sacrificial death and resurrection.**

Have kids turn to John 3:1-17. Assign readers to take the part of the narrator, Nicodemus and Jesus. After reading the passage aloud, have kids gather in a circle and pray sentence prayers of thanks for our hope of eternal life.

ONE TOUGH BATTLE

THEME: Evil

Sometimes evil can seem overpowering. And fighting against it is no easy task. But we can live victoriously when we trust God daily to give us the strength to live a life that honors him. The encouragement from this meeting is that Jesus came to destroy the works of evil—and that kids can share in that "positive destruction."

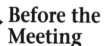 **Before the Meeting**

Gather paper, pencils, markers, continuous-feed computer paper, tape, newspapers and scissors. Be sure everyone will have access to a copy of *The Youth Bible*.

Say: **One of Satan's biggest tricks is to take something that God intended to be good and warp it into something evil.** Let's take a look at what the Bible says about evil, and how we can find the strength to withstand it.

▶ 1. Change for the Worse

Have kids each focus on an item in the room, then think about what might make that object into something evil. For example, curtains could be used by an arsonist to start a fire; a watch could be stolen and hawked at a pawn shop; a shoe could be used to break a window in a robbery. Give kids each a chance to share their ideas.

Ask: **How easy is it to imagine something evil taking place? Explain. How do you feel when you consider the amount of evil in the world? in your friends at school? in yourself? What is the hardest thing about trying to stand against evil or stop it?**

▶ 2. True-to-Life Evil

Form three groups. Assign each group one of the following devotions and passages from *The Youth Bible:* "Quiet Cancer," Genesis 6:5—7:24; "Fearful Escape," Mark 3:20-35; or "Grim Snapshots," Luke 20:9-19. Explain that each group's task is to prepare a report consisting of a summary of the passage and devotion and an answer to the second question in their devotion.

Bring everyone together and have groups share their findings.

Distribute paper and pencils. Have volunteers read aloud "Taking a Stand" and the related passage, Psalm 97.

Based on their insights from Psalm 97, have

kids each jot down brief, experiential definitions of evil. Experiential definitions use action
phrases only. For example, evil is short-chang-
ing a blind man; evil is telling a lie about someone because you're jealous; evil is being glad
when someone gets hurt.

Ask volunteers to read their experiential
definitions.

Ask: **How does reading these definitions
of evil make you feel?**

Invite kids to tell about any real-life experiences they've had that support a particular
definition.

 3. Banner of Hope

Read aloud Romans 12:17-21. Have kids form
two groups. Distribute markers and continuous-
feed computer paper for making banners.

Say: **Group one is going to vote on the
"best" experiential definition of evil and
put it on their banner. Group two will put
the words of Romans 12:21 on theirs.**

After groups have finished, hang the finished
banners side-by-side.

Ask: **How does seeing these two banners
together make you feel? What are some
practical steps we can take to overcome
evil with good?**

 4. Trash the Trash

Distribute scissors and copies of recent newspapers. Have kids each find and cut out one
article that shows some form of evil in the world
today.

Bring everyone together in a circle. Place a
wastebasket in the center. Let kids take turns
sharing the contents of their articles. Ask the
rest of the group to respond with suggestions
about how that evil could be overcome. After
kids have given a response to the evil in each
article, have the student who found that article
rip it up and throw it in the wastebasket.

Ask for closing sentence prayers, thanking
God for his power to overcome evil and making
a commitment to live in his power.

JUST TRUST

THEME: Faith (1)

Faith is a difficult concept for teenagers to grasp. Our technological society teaches kids to base their beliefs on what can be scientifically tested and proven. Kids need to see that human understanding has its God-given limits and that the answers to life's deepest issues can't be reached by the scientific method. This session will help your teenagers evaluate how their faith affects their daily lives.

Before the Meeting

Write the unfinished sentences from activity four on a large sheet of newsprint. Gather paper, pencils and a marker. Make sure everyone has a copy of *The Youth Bible*.

1. Free Fall

Ask for a very trusting volunteer. Have the rest of the kids stand in a tight circle about four feet in diameter. If you have more than eight kids, form two groups. Have the volunteer stand in the middle of the circle with closed eyes, hold a stiff position, and fall back into the arms of the kids in the circle. If the volunteer remains stiff, the others will be able to pass him or her around the circle.

Have the volunteer trade places with someone from the circle, and repeat the fall and pass procedure. Continue until everyone has had a chance to be in the middle.

Ask: **How did you feel just before you allowed yourself to fall? How did it feel to be caught? How is this experience like putting your faith in Jesus? How is it different? What made you decide to believe the group would catch you? What made you decide to believe that Jesus is who he said he is?**

Read aloud the devotion "The Faith Difference" (p. 927 in *The Youth Bible*) and the related scripture passage, Matthew 11:2-11. Discuss the questions at the end of the devotion.

Then say: **We know that our faith is really important to us when it begins to make a significant difference in our daily lives. Let's look at stories of three people and see how their faith affects their lives.**

2. Lives of Faith

Form three groups. Assign one of the following devotions and passages to each group:

"T-e-a-c-h-e-r," Matthew 16:13-20; "Christmas In June, July . . . ," Mark 10:13-16; "Surrender," Luke 7:1-10. Have groups prepare to tell how the characters in their devotions and passages expressed faith.

After a few minutes bring everyone together and have groups share. Then ask: **In what ways have you expressed faith in your life? Do you think faith comes easier to some people than to others? Explain. What makes it difficult to express your faith? What makes it easy?**

▶ 3. Too Good to Be True

Ask: **Have you ever accepted a "free" offer, only to find out later that there were strings attached?**

Allow kids to share their experiences.

Select a story from these devotions in *The Youth Bible*: "Free Approval" (p. 1144) or "You'd Better Believe It!" (p. 1208). Ask someone to read it aloud. Call on two other kids to read aloud Romans 4:1-12 and Galatians 2:11-21.

Ask: **Why is it hard to believe that God's free gift of eternal life is really free? What helps you finally accept God's free gift?**

Lead kids in the first "Consider . . ." idea in "You'd Better Believe It." Distribute pencils and paper. Have kids each make a list of good deeds they've done to try to earn God's acceptance, then tear up the list.

Ask: **How did you feel when you looked at the list of your good deeds and accomplishments? How did it feel to tear up the list? How is tearing up the list like trusting God to love you—no strings attached?**

▶ 4. Faithfully Yours

Give kids each another sheet of paper. Display a large sheet of newsprint with the following unfinished sentences printed on it:

1. My personal definition of faith is . . .
2. It's hardest for me to have faith when . . .
3. Something that builds my faith is . . .
4. One way faith makes a difference in my life is . . .

After kids have completed the sentences have them count off by fours. Have the ones tell how they completed the first sentence, the twos tell how they completed the second sentence, and so on.

Say: **One of our biggest faith-builders is to hear how God works in the lives of others to help them conquer their fears and doubts and come to a point of complete trust. Let's look at another story of a young man who conquered his fears and how that compares to a puzzling experience the disciples had with Jesus.**

▶ 5. Risky Business

Have volunteers read aloud the devotion "Over a Cliff" (p. 980 in *The Youth Bible*) and the related passage, Mark 9:1-9.

Ask: **What physical sensations and emotions do you think Ethan felt as he looked over the cliff? Do you think the disciples at the Transfiguration experienced similar feelings? Explain. When have you experienced those feelings? Do your similar experiences have anything to do with expressing your faith?**

Direct kids' attention to the second "Consider . . ." idea. Have the group brainstorm ways to demonstrate faith, both individually and as a group. Then have kids return to the three groups from activity 2 and share with the others in their groups one way they will personally express their faith this week.

Close with huddle prayers in the three groups, with kids asking God's help for others in the group to express their faith in the ways they've planned.

HOW TO GROW IN FAITH

THEME: Faith (2)

Physical growth is easy to see and measure in teenagers. Spiritual growth is a lot harder to evaluate. During the teen years you may see your teenagers' faith take many dips and curves as kids grapple with their personal beliefs. The good news is that doubts often become stepping stones to greater faith. Use this meeting to help kids discover how faith grows and where they are in the growth process.

▶ Before the Meeting

Gather blindfolds, ice cream, paper cups, spoons, masking tape, marker, construction paper, pencils, a packet of seeds, 3×5 cards, and clear tape. Make sure everyone has a copy of *The Youth Bible*.

▶ 1. Action Faith

Have kids find partners. Give each pair a blindfold, a cup of ice cream and two spoons.

Say: **One partner will put on the blindfold, then feed ice cream to the sighted partner. The sighted partner may not give any directions and has to hold perfectly still while the blindfolded person aims for his or her mouth. The blindfolded person must keep one hand behind his or her back.**

After two minutes have the partners switch roles. After everyone has participated in both roles, have kids remove the blindfolds.

Ask: **How did you feel when you were blindfolded? How did you feel when you could see? Was it easier to feed your partner or be fed? What part did faith play in the blindfold experience? How is having faith in your partner like having faith in God? How is it different?**

▶ 2. Defined Faith

Lay out a Tick-Tack-Toe board on the floor with masking tape. Form two teams. Give one team a stack of X's written on construction paper. Give the other team a stack of O's. Have kids each tape their X or their O to the front of their shirt. Explain that you're going to play Tick-Tack-Toe using questions about faith.

Have teams sit down facing each other on opposite sides of the Tick-Tack-Toe board. Ask a volunteer from one team to read aloud 2 Corinthians 4:13-18 to the whole group. Ask a volunteer from the other team to read aloud Hebrews 11:1-16.

Say: **I'm going to read a series of questions aloud. The first question goes to the X's. The person who answers correctly can occupy any spot on the game board. If the X's answer incorrectly, the O's get a shot. The second question goes to the O's. We'll keep alternating until one team gets three positions in a row on the game board.**

Allow kids to refer to their Bibles as you play. Since some of the questions have personal answers rather than right-or-wrong answers, the competition in the game will center on strategy and placement of players.

Here are the questions for the game.

1. **When have you trusted God even though you didn't know what was going to happen?** (Kids give personal answers.)
2. **According to Hebrews 11, what does faith mean?** (Being sure of the things we hope for; knowing something is real even if we don't see it.)
3. **Why did God call Abel a good man?** (Because of his faith.)
4. **What does everyone need to please God?** (Faith.)
5. **What did Noah hear by faith?** (God's warnings.)
6. **Where did Abraham go by faith?** (To another country.)
7. **Even though the physical body ages, what can be made new each day?** (Our spirit.)
8. **Who is your personal role model in faith?** (Kids give personal answers.)
9. **What does faith give us?** (Hope.)
10. **How will God treat those who truly want to find him?** (He rewards them.)
11. **How does faith help you make it through a hard day?** (Kids give personal answers.)
12. **Why was faith necessary for Abraham to become a father?** (He and Sarah were old.)
13. **What will God do for us that he did for Jesus?** (Raise us from the dead.)
14. **What is God giving to more and more people?** (His grace.)
15. **Why do we have troubles now?** (To help us gain eternal glory.)

Play two or three rounds, then have each team meet and come up with a definition of faith. Bring the whole group together and have teams share their definitions.

▶ 3. Difficult Faith

Have kids form three groups. Assign each group one of the following devotions from *The Youth Bible*: "A Voice in the Dark" (p. 1287), "Stick With It" (p. 1188) and "Unseen Water" (p. 1196).

Allow a few minutes for groups to read their devotions and discuss the questions at the end.

Then bring everyone together and ask: **What was difficult for the character in your story? How did the struggle help your character grow? What experience have you faced that is similar to what this character faced? Did the difficulty you faced help your faith grow? Explain.**

Say: **We all have different experiences and different levels of spiritual growth. Just as we are different physically, we all have strong and weak areas in our spiritual lives as well. The important thing is that we keep on growing.**

▶ 4. Faith Test

Bring all the kids together. Distribute pencils and have kids turn to the devotion "Growing Up" (p. 1128 in *The Youth Bible*) and complete the survey individually.

Say: **Put a star by two or three areas in which you'd like to see your faith grow.**

Then have a volunteer read aloud the related passage, Acts 19:1-7.

Ask: **How did Paul's visit build up the faith of the believers? How does Paul's visit compare to going to a camp or concert or listening to a famous Christian speaker today? What was the attitude of the believers toward Paul? How did their attitude affect the growth of their faith?**

How does our attitude as a group affect our ability to grow in faith?

 5. Growing Faith

Have kids turn to the devotion "It's Alive" (p. 971 in *The Youth Bible*). Ask volunteers to read aloud the story and the accompanying passage, Mark 4:26-34. Then discuss the questions at the end of the devotion.

Lead kids in the second "Consider ..." activity. Direct kids' attention to 2 Peter 1:5-9.

Put a packet of seeds, a stack of 3×5 cards and a roll of clear tape in a central location.

Say: **Take a seed and tape it to a card. Then return to your three groups and brainstorm ways to make your faith grow as Peter describes in these verses. Write on your card one thing you'll do this week to keep your faith growing. Share your plan with the members of your group.**

Gather kids in a circle. Ask individuals to take turns completing this sentence prayer: "Lord, I need you to help me grow in ..."

SURVIVING THE HOME ZONE

THEME: Family

Everyone with a family of any kind has family problems. Teenagers and parents of teenagers face especially tense situations. Kids are focused on gaining their independence, while parents are concerned about keeping sanity and balance in the family as they gradually launch kids into the world. These separate goals often bring parents and kids into direct conflict. In this meeting kids will study scriptural principles and develop practical ideas to increase their sensitivity and skill in dealing with family issues.

▶ Before the Meeting

Photocopy and cut apart the slips from the "Family Assignments" handout. Gather snacks for activity 1, pencils and paper. Make sure you have copies of *The Youth Bible* for everyone.

▶ 1. We Are Family

Form "families" of kids by handing out slips from the "Family Assignments" sheet. Try to use combinations of families that will work out evenly with the number of kids you have. Make extra sets of the assignments if you have more than 25 kids. If kids come in late, have them each join a family as another sibling.

Try to have "mothers" be girls and "fathers" be guys. Siblings can be any combination of genders.

Have kids get together in their families and introduce themselves. Let families each choose their family name and first names for all their members. As people take on their new identities, encourage them to act the ages they've been assigned.

Give each family one fewer snacks than there are family members. For example, a family of five would get four apples. Tell the families to distribute the snack however they want.

After the snacks have been divided and eaten, ask: **How did your family decide to divide up the snacks? Was everyone happy? Why or why not? How well did you feel you worked at resolving the problem? How did it feel being a parent? How did it feel being a child? How is this like what sometimes happens in our real families?**

Say: **You may have guessed that today we're going to be looking at families. Let's learn a little more about them.**

2. Howling at the Moon?

Have all families look up and read the devotion "Sibling Rivalry" (p. 29 in *The Youth Bible*) and the related passage, Genesis 25:19-24. Have families decide whether they agree with the statistics in the devotion, then talk over the questions at the end.

Bring everyone together and ask: **What did your family think about the statistics? Did you all agree? What do you see as the major problems facing families today?**

Now have families all look up and read the devotion "Wolf Packs" (p. 1225 in *The Youth Bible*) and the related passage, Ephesians 6:1-4. Have families discuss the passage and the questions. Then gather everyone together.

Ask: **How might your family better face its problems using the principles in your story and passage?**

3. Family Crisis

Say: **Now we're going to look at some specific family problems.**

Assign each family one of the following devotions and passages from *The Youth Bible*: "Family Feud," Genesis 37:1-36; "A Father's Love," Psalm 127; "Trust," Proverbs 22:1-9. Explain that families are to begin by reading only the devotion. Then they are each to pretend that the situation happened in their family and role play their reactions.

After the role-plays have families each read their scripture passages.

Get the whole group together and ask: **How did your family's reaction to the situation differ from the family in the story? How**

was it the same? **How might your reaction have been different if you'd been following the advice of your scripture passage?**

 ## 4. Live It!

Say: **The Bible gives us lots of guidance about how to live together in a family, but the advice doesn't do much good unless we follow it. In your family, brainstorm six specific ways you can begin to apply some of the scripture you studied or heard about in the last activity.**

Distribute pencils and paper. Give families a couple of minutes, then have them report to the rest of the group. After the reports, have families get together again. Ask kids each to choose one of the suggested ideas to work on in their real families this week. Encourage kids to look at the "Consider . . ." sections of the devotions for even more ideas.

5. Laboratory of Faith

Gather everyone together and have a volunteer read aloud the devotion "Laboratory of Faith" (p. 1005 in *The Youth Bible*) and the accompanying scripture passage, Luke 2:22-40. Discuss the first two questions as a group. Then ask the last questions and let kids think about them.

Have kids return to their families to wrap up the session. Encourage kids who feel comfortable doing so to share their real-life family problems and pray about them together.

Encourage today's families to support and pray for each other in the coming week.

WE ARE

FAMILY ASSIGNMENTS

Family A
Mother

Family A
13-year-old

Family A
16-year-old

Family B
Father

Family B
Mother

Family B
14-year-old

Family B
16-year-old

Family C
Father

Family C
Mother

Family C
10-year-old

Family C
14-year-old

Family C
15-year-old

Family C
17-year-old

FAMILY

Family D
Mother

Family D
12-year-old

Family D
15-year-old

Family D
16-year-old

Family E
Father

Family E
13-year-old

Family E
18-year-old

Family F
Father

Family F
Mother

Family F
15-year-old

Family F
14-year-old

Family F
14-year-old

WHO'S AFRAID OF THE BIG, BAD WORLD?

THEME: Fear

Any big, bad wolves in your life? We all have fears. Even the most confident people in the world have fears deep down. Some of our fears are justified; others aren't. But whether fears are justified or not makes little difference to the person experiencing them—they're real fears either way. Help your kids find ways to face their fears by seeing how biblical people confronted fears that faced them.

▶ Before the Meeting

For every three or four kids, you'll need a bag of popped popcorn and an empty 2-liter bottle. You'll also need newsprint, markers and a copy of *The Youth Bible* for each group member.

▶ 1. Pushing Popcorn

Tell kids you're going to have a contest. Form teams of three or four and give each team a soft drink bottle and a bag of popped popcorn. Explain that the goal is to get as much popcorn in the bottle as they can in one minute.

Say: **There'll be no big winner, but the team with the least amount of popcorn in its bottle when I call time will have to run around the church building three times.**

Let teams start together. Keep time, and start counting down the seconds by fives when you reach the last 30 seconds. Count down the last 10 seconds one at a time. While kids are stuffing popcorn in the bottles, remind them of the penalty for finishing last.

When you call time, line up the bottles and make a big production of declaring the losing team.

Then say: **I was just joking. You really don't have to run around the church. In fact, because you're such good losers, you get to eat your popcorn.**

Let all the kids begin eating the popcorn, then ask: **How did you feel while you were racing to stuff popcorn in your bottle? Do you ever feel anxious and afraid about things in real life? How is that like how you felt in this activity? Those of you who lost, how did you feel when I said you didn't have to run? How is that like how you feel in real** life when a source of fear is taken away?

Say: **Today we're talking about fear. We're going to look at fears some other people have and how they overcome them. And we're going to take a look at how we can overcome fears too.**

2. Calm and Cool?

Choose two good readers to read John 18:1-27 aloud together. Before you have them read, instruct the rest of your kids to act like kids their age might act if someone stood on the street and read aloud from the Bible. Encourage kids to be rude and ridicule the readers like kids at school would.

When the reading is finished, ask the readers: **How did it feel being ridiculed? How is that like the feeling you get when you think you should take a stand that might be unpopular with your friends? How are those fears similar to Peter's?**

3. Drowning in Fear

Ask: **What fears do Christian teenagers have today?**

After a few minutes of discussion, read aloud "The Handicap" (p. 935 in *The Youth Bible*) and have kids follow along. Then read the related scripture passage, Matthew 14:22-33, and discuss the questions at the end of the story.

Then ask: **Why didn't Peter drown? How does Jesus save us when we're fearful in tough situations?**

Begin the first "Consider . . ." activity together. Put up a sheet of newsprint, divide it down the center, and have kids list fears teenagers face. Start with suggestions from your previous discussion.

When kids have listed all the fears they can think of, brainstorm ways to overcome the fears. Encourage kids to think about the scriptures they've studied today.

4. Pair Prayers

Continue the first "Consider . . ." activity from p. 935. Form pairs and have partners discuss the fears on the list that concern them the most. Encourage kids to be honest and kind.

After kids have shared, say: **One way to overcome our fears is to share them with people who care about us—like we just did. Others can help us find solutions to our problems and can point us to scriptures that may be helpful. And sometimes just telling someone else about a fear makes it seem a little less frightening.**

5. David's Prayer

Say: **There are times we all think we're the only person on earth who has such fears. But everyone has fears. Let's look at one prominent Christian from the past whose fear might surprise you.**

Read "An Antidote for Fear" and Psalm 27 (p. 497 in *The Youth Bible*). When you get to the questions, stop reading. Ask for several volunteers to read Psalm 27 aloud. Assign each reader one or more verses. Give readers a minute to read through their verses silently.

Say: **Our reading of this psalm will be the closing prayer for our class. Let's all listen and lift our thanks and praise to God together.**

Encourage your readers to read with the feeling David might have had when he wrote the psalm.

When the reading is finished, pause before saying "amen" and dismissing the group.

LIVING ON THE EDGE

THEME: Following God (1)

Many people liken Christianity to a mean old Aunt who won't let them have any fun. They see the Bible as a list of do's and don'ts. In reality, the opposite is true: The Bible is a guidebook that points the way to enjoying life to the full. The don'ts are warning signs that help us avoid getting into traps or crossing boundaries that lead to bad times.

This meeting challenges kids to see God's Word in a new light—not as a rope that ties them off from fun times, but as an arrow that points to what life is really all about.

▶ Before the Meeting

On a sheet of newsprint, write the devotions and scripture passages for activity 2, then tape the sheet to the wall. Gather rope, string or measuring tape; paper; pencils; and extra copies of *The Youth Bible*.

▶ 1. Fun Within Limits

Have kids gather in the center of the room.

Ask: **How little floor space do you think this group could take up?**

Get kids to make guesses about how many feet the circumference of a circle around the group might be. After several guesses, find out whose guess came closest by having everyone squeeze together as tight as possible. Place a rope circle on the floor around them.

Before removing the rope to measure it, say: **While I've got you here, let's do something fun. Without leaving the circle, try waltzing with someone next to you.**

After several people fall outside the circle, gather the rope and measure it to see whose guess was closest.

Congratulate the winner, then ask: **How did you feel being squeezed in close boundaries? How is this like some people look at the Christian life? Why do some people fall away from following Jesus, the way some of you fell out of the circle?**

Say: **Many people think Christians can't have any fun, but actually the opposite is true. There can be no lasting fun without Jesus. Let's look at a story about someone who dealt with this issue.**

▶ 2. Christianity in Court

Read aloud the devotion "The Fun Factor" (p. 1271 in *The Youth Bible*).

Ask: **Suppose you were a defense lawyer**

given the task of finding "evidence" in an upcoming court battle that accuses Christians of being boring. What evidence could you find—in the Bible and in your experience—that shows how the "rules" of Christianity actually lead to greater happiness and fun. Could you do it? Let's find out.

Form two teams—the prosecution and the defense. Point out devotions and passages you wrote on newsprint before the meeting: "A Trusted Leader," Exodus 19:1-8; "His Presence," Job 42:1-6; "To Live in Freedom," Psalm 119:33-48; "Bouncing Betties," Romans 12:1-16; "Daring to Believe," 2 Corinthians 5:6-17; and "The Fun Factor," Titus 2:11—3:7.

Have teams each prepare their case. Encourage the defense to emphasize how these scriptures point the way to freedom and fun. Encourage the prosecution to emphasize how these passages restrict people from doing whatever makes them feel good.

When teams are ready, have them take turns presenting their cases, then allow a short time for open debate. After the debate, have everyone act as part of the "jury" and vote on which position was right.

Say: **When you look at the Bible critically, it's easy to see that it's far more than just a list of mindless do's and don'ts. It's God's handbook for showing us how to find true happiness and fulfillment. Unfortunately, we don't always follow God's ways. Let's do an activity to see how well we've held to the life God wants us to live.**

▶ 3. Lord of the Past

Have kids turn to "Where Am I?" (p. 685 in *The Youth Bible*). Invite them each to do the "Consider . . ." exercise—creating a timeline of their lives that shows when they have felt lost and when they have followed God.

Hand out paper and pencils and allow several minutes for kids to work.

When everyone is finished, ask: **What's one time in your life you really followed God? How did you feel about following God at that time? What's one time in your life you didn't follow God? What was your life like then? When are you happier—when you follow God or when you don't? How does this influence how you think about the do's and don'ts of the Bible? What can you do this week to seek out the true happiness God offers through his Word?**

▶ 4. Spin-Out

Have kids stand in a circle and close their eyes. Instruct everyone to spin around three times and try to end up facing you. After the big spin-out, have all the kids open their eyes at once and take note of the direction they're facing.

Say: **Without God's guidance, we are like wanderers without a compass, bouncing around without direction. People in that circumstance might look free, but they're really lost and will eventually end up in despair. When we follow God, we learn what it means to live life to the full. And because we have direction and purpose, we can avoid the traps life holds and find all that makes life really worth living.**

Close with prayer, thanking God for guiding kids to true fulfillment in life.

TUNING IN TO GOD

THEME: Following God (2)

Sometimes following God is less a matter of obedience than awareness. A lot of Christian teenagers are willing to do what God wants—the problem is that they seldom stop to think about what God's will is. This meeting will help kids think about what they can do to be more "tuned in" to God on a daily basis.

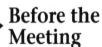

Before the Meeting

Prepare a series of math problems as described in activity 1. Gather 3×5 cards, pencils, paper, newsprint and markers. Make sure each student has a copy of *The Youth Bible*.

▶ 1. Math Concentration

Form pairs and distribute 3×5 cards and pencils. Tell kids they'll be playing a game of Arithmetic Elimination. For each round, have pairs designate one partner as the concentrator and the other as the distracter. Have partners alternate roles as the rounds progress. If you have an uneven number of kids, form one group of three in which two kids will act as distracters.

Prepare about 15 math problems of increasing difficulty. For example, start with something like "(7+3)×5." Then create longer and longer strings for later problems, such as "(1+8-2)×3+15." As you read each problem aloud to the group, have the concentrators try to solve it in their heads, while the distracters whisper random numbers in the concentrators' ears. Be sure the same kids aren't distracters from round to round.

Before you announce each answer, have the concentrators jot down their answers on 3×5 cards. Have each concentrator who answered incorrectly leave the game. Have the remaining kids form new pairs and start round two. Continue until only two people remain—one concentrator and one distracter. Have them alternate roles to see who will be eliminated first. The remaining player is the winner.

After the game, ask: **How did you feel trying to think through these problems with someone trying to distract you? What would have made the game easier? How is this exercise like the challenge of listening to God and living the Christian life? What kinds of distractions might keep you from** following God fully?

Say: **Excelling at anything—including the Christian life—requires determination and concentration. Let's look at a story that illustrates this point.**

▶ 2. Concentration Factor

Have a volunteer read aloud "Life at the Top" (p. 1318 in *The Youth Bible*).

Say: **Lynn's experience with mountain climbing is a good illustration of the concentration required to excel at anything worthwhile. Let's think some more about what might hinder our ability to focus on God's will for our lives.**

Form four groups (a group can be one person) and assign each group one of the following devotions and passages from *The Youth Bible*: "Totally Committed," Deuteronomy 6:1-9; "Tuned In," Matthew 13:1-23; "Wake Up!" Colossians 3:1-10; or "Get Ready!" 1 Thessalonians 5:1-11.

Have each group read through the devotion and passage, then discuss the questions at the end. Tell kids to watch for things that help us follow God or distract us from following him. Then bring everyone together and have groups share their findings.

Ask: **What's the biggest help to you in trying to focus on following God? What's your biggest distraction?**

▶ 3. Poetic Awareness

Say: **Getting people to "tune in" to something can be hard, especially if you only have a few words to grab their attention. We're going to write simple three-line poems that express new ways for us to tune in to God.**

Distribute paper and pencils. Write this sample on a sheet of newsprint:

Answering machines
Never miss a call.
I'm trying to catch your messages, Lord.

Say: **Don't be nervous about writing this poem, because I'm going to give instructions for each line.**

Pause and allow writing time between each of the following instructions:

- Line 1: Write the name of some kind of communication equipment.
- Line 2: Express what that equipment does.
- Line 3: Tell how you will respond to God in a similar manner.

When everyone has finished, ask for volunteers to share their poems. Praise kids for their creativity.

Say: **The more "tuned in" to God we become, the easier it is for us to discover his will for our lives.**

▶ 4. Prayers of Listening

Have kids sit on the floor, putting as much distance as possible between themselves and the other kids.

Say: **In our group we've prayed in many different ways for many different things. Today I want us to pray prayers of listening for God's guidance. Concentrate on the Bible passages we've studied and be still before God for a few moments.**

After two or three minutes, close in prayer, asking God to help kids be sensitive to his guidance.

STICKING IT OUT

THEME: Following God (3)

Why do so few people make it to the Olympics? No doubt natural ability plays a part, but the bottom line is that there are only a few people who have the determination and endurance and are willing to make the sacrifice and commitment it takes to become one of the best athletes in the world.

Sadly, the same is often true in the Christian realm. Following God requires all the grit of an Olympic hopeful, but often we're tempted to lay aside our deeper commitments when they require more of us than we want to give. This meeting challenges kids to take a look at their lifestyles to see if they've got what it takes to follow God—no matter what the cost.

▶ Before the Meeting

Label five paper bags for the excuse contest in activity 1. Hide an 8- to 16-foot 2×4 in the room, to use in activity 4. Gather 3×5 cards, pencils, masking tape, newsprint, a marker and a blindfold. Make sure everyone has a copy of *The Youth Bible*.

▶ 1. Excuse Contest

Distribute pencils and 3×5 cards and tell kids they are going to enter an Excuse Contest, based on a story you'll read to them. Tell kids their excuses will be voted on in each of the following categories: Most Wild and Crazy Excuse, Most Believable Excuse, Most Unbelievable Excuse, Most Childish Excuse and Most Dull Excuse.

Set out five paper bags, each labeled with one of the categories. Then read aloud this story:

You just got your drivers license. Your parent loans you the car after you explain that you want to go to a special meeting at church. The guest speaker is a woman missionary from Brazil. Your parent says you can go straight there and back, and you promise to be home by 8:30 p.m.

You arrive home at 1 a.m. Your parent is very anxious and looks at the car for damage. The right fender is dented, with pieces of seaweed hanging from the bumper. Bits of popcorn lay scattered in the back seat, and a smudge of lipstick is found on the dashboard. Your parent asks you what happened, and this is the excuse you give . . .

Tell kids to write out a detailed excuse on

their cards. When everyone is finished, have kids toss their cards into a pile in the center of the room. Collect the cards, shuffle them, and read them aloud to the group. After you read each card, have the group vote on which category the excuse best fits. Then drop the excuse in the appropriate bag.

After all the cards are read, have kids vote on the best excuse in each category.

Congratulate the winners, then ask: **How does it feel when you make excuses about something you've done? What's the easiest thing about making excuses? the hardest? Why are we tempted to make excuses to God for our actions or our lack of action?**

Say: **People started making excuses to God long before any of us were born. In fact, the art goes as far back as Adam himself. Let's look at some other characters who made excuses to God.**

▶ 2. Challenging Discoveries

Form three groups and assign each group one of the following devotions from *The Youth Bible*: "When the Going Gets Tough ..." (p. 1280), "The Choice to Follow" (p. 1034) or "Standing Alone" (p. 1329).

Have groups think of excuses the characters in their stories could have used to get out of trouble. When kids are ready, bring everyone together and have each group briefly tell its story and give the possible excuses.

Ask: **What are some other common excuses people use for not following God?**

Say: **Let's see how some Bible characters handled excuses.**

Tape a sheet of newsprint to the wall and write on it the following headings: Scripture, Character(s), Challenge and Possible Excuse. Have kids return to their groups. Assign each group two of the following passages: Jeremiah 7:1-15 and Hosea 6:1-6; Matthew 1:18-25 and Mark 1:14-20; or Luke 14:25-30 and Acts 9:1-10.

Say: **As you read these passages, determine the characters involved, the challenge to those characters, and what possible excuse those characters might have given to**

avoid the situation.

When groups are ready, have them report on their findings.

Ask: **How are the challenges you face in following God today like the challenges these Bible characters faced? What excuses might you use to get out of really living the Christian life?**

Say: **There are lots of ways to avoid the challenge of the Christian walk if we want to. But when we make excuses, we're really showing that we can't put our faith where our mouths are. Let me illustrate what I mean.**

▶ 3. Talk or Walk?

Have a volunteer read aloud "Show and Tell" (p. 1112 in *The Youth Bible*).

After the reading, say: **To bring the point of this story home, let's set up our own balancing challenge. Suppose I were to lay a 2×4 down on the floor in front of you. How many of you think you would be able to stand on it for five seconds without falling off? walk across it? cross it blindfolded? cross it backwards, blindfolded? cross it backwards, blindfolded, and hopping on one foot? cross it backwards, blindfolded, hopping on one foot, with your hands clasped behind your back? How strongly do you believe you could do what you said you could?**

After a show of hands, bring out the 2×4 and say: **Here's your chance to walk your talk!**

Have all who raised their hands attempt to walk along the board as they promised. Praise kids for their efforts.

Ask: **What's the difference between saying you believe something and living it out? How are excuses related to living (or not living) out your faith?**

▶ 4. Commitment Challenge

Say: **Let's close our meeting by making a commitment to live out all that we say we believe about Jesus and to stop making**

excuses when the challenge gets tough.

Have kids stand in a line on top of the 2×4. Larger groups may need to form a circle around it. Close in silent prayer, encouraging kids to tell God about their commitments to live what they believe and to support each other when the challenge to "stay on board" gets difficult.

THE TWO SIDES OF FORGIVENESS

THEME: Forgiveness

Forgiveness has two sides for us as humans: seeking forgiveness and forgiving others. God expects us to do both. Help your kids see how asking for forgiveness and forgiving others are two sides of the same coin, and the basis for establishing healthy relationships with people and with God.

▶ Before the Meeting

You'll need a roll of masking tape, two softball-size Nerf balls, chairs, spoons, paper and pencils. Make sure everyone has a copy of *The Youth Bible*.

▶ 1. To Forgive or Not to Forgive

Read aloud the first section of the devotion "So Sorry" (p. 941 in *The Youth Bible*) through the sentence ending "she snapped."

Then ask: **Should Matt forgive Lisa? Why or why not?**

Let kids discuss their ideas.

Then say: **This meeting is on forgiveness. It's not always easy to forgive or to ask for forgiveness, but we're going to look at examples that show us why it's best to forgive.**

▶ 2. Foam-Ball Trouble

Form two teams. Give each team a softball-size Nerf ball. Put a masking tape line on the floor at one end of the room and place a chair at the other end of the room. Have the teams line up behind the line. Hand the first member of each team a spoon and place a ball on each spoon.

Say: **On "go," put one hand behind your back and race around the chair back to your team. Give the next person the spoon and ball without removing your hand from behind your back. Keep going until everyone has raced around the chair. The first team to finish wins.**

Say "go," but as soon as someone drops the ball, stop the race.

Say: **Oh, I didn't tell you. If a team drops the ball it's automatically disqualified. The other team wins.**

Have kids sit down. Everyone will probably see this as a botched activity, and kids from the disqualified team are likely to be angry.

Ask: **How do you feel about what we just did? Will you forgive me for not telling you about dropping the ball? How is this like or unlike your feelings when a friend does something that makes you angry?**

▶ 3. Fume or Forgive?

Look again at the "So Sorry" devotion on p. 941 of *The Youth Bible*. Read aloud the rest of the devotion and the related scripture, Matthew 18:21-35. Discuss the questions at the end of the devotion.

Say: **There are two sides to forgiveness: forgiving others and receiving forgiveness. Refusing to forgive can cause terrible problems within a friendship. And receiving forgiveness can remove our guilt. Let's see more of what the Bible says about forgiveness.**

▶ 4. Prescriptions for Forgiveness

Form two groups. Assign the following devotions and passages from *The Youth Bible* to the groups.

Group 1: "An Unexpected Visitor," Ezra 9:1-9; "Change of Heart," Joel 2:12-19; "Personal Peace," Jonah 3:1-10; "The Christmas Gift," Mark 2:1-12; and "The Face of Hatred," Colossians 1:15-29.

Group 2: "Living With Consequences," Exodus 34:4-8; "Lasting Impact," Luke 23:26-43; "Only a Car," Romans 3:21-28; "Putting Up Bail" Ephesians 1:1-10; and "Accidents Happen," 1 Timothy 1:12-17.

Give each group a pencil and a slip of paper on which to write a "prescription." Have group 1 write a prescription for healing relationships through forgiving. Have group 2 write a prescription for receiving healing through seeking forgiveness.

Give groups about 15 minutes to read their devotions and passages, discuss the questions

and write their prescriptions.

Then bring everyone together and have groups report on what they've written. If you have time, you might have groups switch passages and write new prescriptions before reporting.

After groups have reported, summarize their presentations.

▶ 5. A Time to Forgive?

Say: **Most likely, our discussion today has brought someone to your mind—either someone you need to forgive or someone you need to ask forgiveness from. Let's take a few minutes right now for some directed prayers. I'll suggest things for you to pray about, then give you a chance to do it.**

Lead the directed prayer with the following statements, allowing about a minute between each one:

- Ask God's forgiveness for times you've wronged him.
- Ask God to help you forgive people for specific wrongs they've done to you.
- Ask God to help you think of people you need to ask forgiveness from because of wrongs you've done them.

After the prayer, have kids each look back at the devotions they've read today and choose one "Consider..." action to do this week. Have them each mark it in their Bible and commit to following through on it this week.

▶ 6. Cleansed!

Form a circle. Have someone read aloud 1 John 1:9.

Ask: **What does this scripture mean for us? How many times will God forgive us? What sins will he not forgive?**

After assuring kids that God will forgive us whenever we sincerely confess our sin and turn from it, close your meeting with prayer, thanking God for his mercy and forgiveness.

Just for fun, you might want to have kids play the foam-ball game again—only this time, be more forgiving when the ball is dropped!

CAN YOU HANDLE IT?

THEME: Freedom

Freedom is more than doing whatever you want to do. Freedom is "from" something, but it is also "to" something. With freedom comes responsibility. This meeting will help the kids in your group understand the benefits as well as the responsibilities that come with true freedom.

▶ Before the Meeting

Gather supplies for one or two of the options in activity 1. For option A you'll need a wheelchair. For option B gather several pairs of old eyeglasses, a black marker, about two dozen buttons and several 18-inch lengths of string. For option C gather a couple of hand-held mirrors, pencils and paper.

You'll also need newsprint, masking tape, 3×5 cards and a copy of *The Youth Bible* for each group member.

▶ 1. Disability Captivity

Option A: *If you have a wheelchair*—Let kids take turns sitting in the wheelchair. Have them attempt the following tasks without help: entering the building, entering and exiting the restroom, finding a place to sit in the sanctuary where they won't be conspicuous, getting a drink of water, washing their hands at a sink.

Option B: *If you have old eyeglasses*—Use the marker to paint a black dot about the size of a dime in the middle of each lens. Have kids wear these glasses while they try to thread several buttons onto a piece of string.

Option C: *If you have hand-held mirrors*—Have kids write their names and addresses on pieces of paper, as straight and as neatly as possible. The catch is that they are only allowed to look at the papers as they are reflected in the mirror.

After the activity, gather the kids in a circle.

Ask: **What kinds of feelings did you have as you tried to do this task? What was the most frustrating?**

Explain that the activity gave a brief experiential introduction to the limitations experienced by people with certain kinds of physical disabilities: The wheelchair demonstrated paraplegia; the eyeglasses gave an idea of what it's like to have cataracts; the mirror-writing showed something of what it's like to have dyslexia.

Ask: **Suppose you had lived with one of these disabilities all your life; then a doc-**

tor came and offered to free you from your condition in exchange for your most valuable possession. What would you trade for that freedom?

Say: **Usually we associate captivity with jails and prisons, but there are other kinds of captivity. You have just experienced some of them. Let's look a little more closely at the nature of freedom from the Bible's perspective.**

 2. Two-Sided Freedom

Form groups of three or more. Assign one or two of the following devotions and passages from *The Youth Bible* to each group: "A Place to Call Home," Exodus 14:19-31; "Tearing Down the Walls," Isaiah 52:1-10; "Going to a Safe Place," Matthew 2:13-23; "Free to Choose," Mark 2:23—3:6; "A Slave to Freedom," Romans 6:1-12; "Free to Do Good," 1 Corinthians 8:1-13. (You don't have to use all the passages.)

Draw a line down the middle of a large sheet of newsprint. On the left side write "From." On the right side write "To."

Say: **In each of these devotions a person is freed from something. But being freed** *from* **something also means being freed** *to* **something. For instance, the freedom that comes with driving also carries with it the responsibility for the safety of your passengers and other drivers on the road. As you go through your devotions and passages, look for what the characters are set free from and what they are set free to do.**

Give groups a few minutes to read and discuss their devotions and passages. Then bring everyone together. As kids share what their characters were freed from and what they were freed

to do, record their findings on the newsprint.

Say: **God, in his love, gives us freedom. But with each freedom comes responsibility. With each of the freedoms listed here on the newsprint comes a responsibility for, or to, something or somebody.**

Ask: **In your opinion, could anyone ever have complete freedom with no responsibility? Explain.**

▶ **3. Looking at Limits**

Distribute 3×5 cards. Have kids turn to "A Slave to Freedom" (p. 1147 in *The Youth Bible*) and read the first item under "Consider ..."

Say: **As we get older, we get more freedom. But we also have to take on more responsibility. What freedom are you really looking forward to or wishing would be granted to you? Jot it down on your card.**

After kids have written their responses, have them find partners. One partner will read the desired freedom, and the other will role play a parent's response. Explain that the role-plays should indicate what limits or duties the parents might suggest to go along with the proposed freedoms.

▶ **4. Prayer Power**

Have kids stay with their partners.

Say: **Share two things with your partner. First, tell about a freedom you're really thankful to have. Second, tell about one freedom you sometimes have trouble handling. Then pray together, praising God for the freedoms you talked about and asking his help in using those freedoms wisely.**

STICK WITH IT!

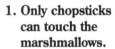

THEME: Friends (1)

Friends are friends forever, the song says. That may be true, but sometimes friends—even the Christian variety—can feel like enemies. Misunderstandings and feelings of betrayal are bound to be part of any long-term friendship. Society urges kids to walk away from difficult relationships. But scripture says *love, understand, forgive, work it out.*

This meeting reviews the dynamics of friendship, both the pleasant and the painful. Kids will learn that true friends stick with each other, even when times get tough.

Before the Meeting

Cut five "bumper stickers" from construction paper. Gather enough chopsticks for each person to have one, one or more bags of marshmallows (depending on the size of your group), paper plates, markers, a 20-foot piece of rope or clothesline, paper, pencils and envelopes. Make sure you have a copy of *The Youth Bible* for each student.

1. Chop-Stick-Together

Announce a Chinese Marshmallow-Eating Contest. Explain that the marshmallows are not Chinese, but the method of eating them *is*. Have kids sit in a circle. Put a paper plate full of marshmallows within reach of every two or three kids. Hand each kid one chopstick.

Say: **The person who eats the most marshmallows in three minutes will be the winner. These are the rules:**

1. Only chopsticks can touch the marshmallows.
2. You can hold only one chopstick.
3. No stabbing or poking the marshmallow.
4. No scooping, rolling or picking up the plate.

These rules should make it impossible to pick up a marshmallow with only one chopstick. Start the activity and let kids work at it until somebody gets the idea of cooperating as partners and squeezing the marshmallow between their two chopsticks. As soon as the idea catches on, the race will heat up. Be sure to keep the paper plates supplied with marshmallows.

If no one gets the idea of cooperating with a partner, say: **Remember, I never said it was illegal to use more than one chopstick—you just can't hold more than one yourself.** If you have a winner, reward him or her with "a year's supply of chopsticks"—all the chopsticks you used in the activity.

Ask: **Who got the idea of helping another person pick up a marshmallow? How did you decide who got to eat the marshmallow? How did it feel to give up your chance to win for your partner? Did anybody get "betrayed"—that is, you helped someone else eat, but then they wouldn't help you? How did that feel? How would that be similar to being betrayed in a friendship? Can any of you tell about that kind of experience?**

Explain that you'll be dealing with the topic of friendship during this meeting—both the good and the painful feelings it can bring.

▶ 2. Pain or Solarcaine?

Ask kids to name some good things that can come from friendships and some of the painful things that can happen too.

Say: **We're all aware that friendships give us a lot of comfort and good feelings, but sometimes friends can "burn" us too. We could say that in friendship there is potential for both pain (like a sunburn—ouch!) and Solarcaine (good, soothing feelings of being liked and cared for). Let's look at some Bible passages and identify the pain and Solarcaine friendship dynamics we find.**

Form groups of three or more. Assign each group one of the following devotions and passages from *The Youth Bible*: "Betrayed," Psalm 55; "Diary of a Backstabber," Matthew 26:14-25; "Helping Each Other," Luke 17:1-10; "The Tough Choice," John 13:31-35; "When Friends Fail," Galatians 6:1-10. (You don't have to use all the passages.)

Give groups each a marker and a construction paper "bumper sticker." Explain that they are to do three tasks: (1) read the material aloud together; (2) decide if the devotion is mostly focused on Pain or Solarcaine, and tell why; and (3) create a group bumper sticker that sums up a key theme in their devotion.

Allow 10 or 15 minutes for groups to complete their tasks. Then pull everyone together and have groups each share their bumper sticker

and give a brief explanation of their devotion.

Ask: **What mistakes or wrong decisions can people make that bring pain into an otherwise healthy relationship? What can be done to bring healing to a burned-out relationship? Use the situations in your devotions to give specific examples.**

▶ 3. On the Line for a Friend

Lay the piece of clothesline on the floor in a straight line across the room, then read aloud the vignette about Keivan in the devotion "A Way Out" (p. 1125 in *The Youth Bible*).

Ask: **Why do you think Conrad came to Keivan's rescue? Would you agree that sometimes we need to put ourselves on the line for a friend? What's your experience with this?**

After some sharing, tell kids you're going to read three situations. After each one, they will decide whether or not they would choose to put themselves on the line for their friend in that situation.

Say: **If you would be willing to stand up for your friend, then literally put yourself "on the line" by standing on this piece of clothesline. Then tell what you would do to support your friend and why.**

Here are the situations:

1. **You convinced your summer-job boss to hire your friend Danny, even though Danny was fired from his last job. Danny assured you that he would work hard and be responsible. Danny works for two days, then fails to show up for the next three days. You call him at noon and find he's at home, drunk. Your boss asks, "What happened to your friend?" Would you put yourself on the line for Danny? How?**

2. **Jane told her history teacher, Mr. Simpson, that her research paper would be turned in next Tuesday. But Jane tells you on Friday that she hasn't even started on the paper. She asks if she can use your history paper from last semester as "a**

reference" over the weekend. Do you put yourself on the line for Jane? How?

3. You are walking home from school with Sam. Another guy from your class, Ted, is just a few steps in front of you. Sam makes a couple of loud comments about Ted's immature lunchroom behavior. Sam didn't realize that Ted was into judo. Ted jumps Sam and starts beating him up pretty badly. You're watching this horrible scene unfold. Do you put yourself on the line for Sam? How?

▶ **4. Coping with Conflict**

The situations above raise questions about how to resolve conflict in a friendship. In your closing moments, focus on "I Hate You" (p. 940 in *The Youth Bible*). After reading the devotion aloud, distribute paper, pencils and envelopes. Invite kids to work on the first "Consider ..." idea—developing a list of friends with whom they have conflicts and praying for help to deal with the situations. Have kids each write their name on their envelope, put their list inside, and seal the envelope.

Say: **I'm going to put these envelopes in a confidential file and give them back to you in two months so you can check on how you're doing in resolving these conflicts.**

Close in prayer asking God's wisdom and patience as you work through the conflicts that arise in your relationships.

REACH OUT

THEME: Friends (2)

Birds of a feather flock together often becomes our guiding principle in choosing friends. We want to see our kids build safe, wholesome relationships with other teenagers. But radically different principles flow from the scriptures. Jesus included unwanted people from the backwash of society in his close relationships.

Being a friend sometimes means reaching out and including those who are different. This meeting will encourage your kids to look beyond their comfort zones for friendship and to think about the role commitment plays in meaningful relationships.

▶ Before the Meeting

Make a photocopy of the handout "The Search for Mr. and Ms. Most-Like-Everybody-Else" for each person in attendance. Gather pencils, a small garden shovel, a football and a large cardboard carton. Make sure everyone has a copy of *The Youth Bible*.

▶ 1. The Same Game

Distribute pencils and the handout "The Search for Mr. and Ms. Most-Like-Everybody-Else." Have kids fill it out.

Then say: **This is a game about being the same. You're going to match your survey with as many people as you can in 10 minutes. Both you and the person you're talking to get a plus point each time you find something in common. You both receive a minus point if you discover differences. At** the end, I'll give you a chance to total your points, and we'll find out who's more like everybody than anybody else!

Encourage kids to circulate and talk with as many people as possible in the time allowed. Then give them a moment to add their plus points and subtract their minus points to come up with a grand total. Announce a winner or winners.

Say: **What's good about being pretty much the same as your friends? What's good about being different? In your opinion, are the strongest friendships usually based on similarities or differences? When you choose friends, do you usually look for people who are a lot like you? Explain.**

▶ 2. Reach Out

Say: **The devotions we'll be looking at have to do with accepting others. As Chris-**

tians, we're called to accept other people, even when they're different. We're talking about tough stuff here—reaching out to difficult people, to outsiders and to those who are usually shunned by popular kids.

Have kids form groups of three to five. Assign each group one of the following devotions and passages from *The Youth Bible*: "A Little Encouragement," Ruth 1:1-19; "Everyone Welcome (Almost)," Psalm 69:6-15; "A New Kind of Friend," Luke 14:7-14; "Accepted," Romans 15:4-13; "Inside Lingo," 1 Corinthians 14:13-20; or "A Friend in Everyone," Philemon 4-21. (You don't have to use all the passages.)

Say: **Read your devotion and Bible passage, then be ready to report to the whole group how they illustrate a Christian response to accepting others.** After a few minutes, bring everyone together and ask groups to report on their findings.

Ask: **Why is it so hard for us to reach out to people who are different? What risks are involved in looking for friends outside our own group? Why should we take those risks?**

▶ **3. You Call the Play**

Have kids turn to "First-String Help" (p. 1229 in *The Youth Bible*). Read Philippians 1:3-11 and briefly explain its context and main point. Then ask for volunteers to read the parts of the narrator, Wyatt, Steve, Todd's mom and the football coach.

After the reading, say: **This story really makes the point that friendship equals commitment. But the various people in the story may interpret that principle differently, depending on their point of view. How would each character respond to the idea: Friendship equals commitment?** Ask the kids who read the various parts to role play

their reactions to Wyatt's decision.

Have kids form a circle. Place a football and a small gardening shovel in the center.

Say: **Put yourself in Wyatt's shoes. If you would've stayed with the football team, come huddle around the football. If you would've dropped out to help Todd, come huddle around the shovel.**

Give kids a moment to make their choices. Then have the two groups sit down. Ask the kids in the football group to toss the football to each other and explain their choices as they hold the football. Have the kids in the other group carefully do the same with the shovel.

Ask: **What makes this such a hard decision? Do you think Wyatt will regret his choice later on? Why or why not? As Christian friends, can we expect this kind of commitment from each other?**

▶ **4. Fond Farewells**

Say: **We want to show our commitment and appreciation to our good friends while we have them, because the day will come when we'll have to say goodbye—sometimes sooner than we think.**

Ask someone to read aloud "Saying Good-Bye" (p. 333 in *The Youth Bible*).

Bring out the large cardboard carton and ask the person who reads the story aloud to stand inside it. Explain that the box represents packing up and moving away. Ask kids to think about what they would want to say if that person were moving away tomorrow. Have everyone in the group take a turn standing in the box and receiving fond farewells from the group.

Close by standing in a circle and singing the song "Friends" from *The Group Songbook* (Group Books).

THE SEARCH FOR MR. & MS. MOST-LIKE-EVERYBODY-ELSE

Name _____

Fill out this survey by writing down three things under each category. Then match up your survey with as many others as you can before time is called. Give yourself a plus point each time something on your list matches something on another person's list. (For instance, you are both in band or you both wear glasses.) Give yourself a minus point every time you find something different. (For instance, you listed ice cream, but the other person didn't.)

PLUS POINTS   MINUS POINTS

SCHOOL ACTIVITIES

1.

2.

3.

CLOTHES/APPEARANCE

1.

2.

3.

HOBBIES

1.

2.

3.

MUSIC (top three favorite groups)

1.

2.

3.

FOOD (top three favorites)

1.

2.

3.

YOUR GRAND TOTAL (subtract minus points from plus points): _____

DIRECTING DESTINY

THEME: Future

The future is a hard thing for kids to picture. Until they near the end of high school, many kids rarely think of anything beyond tomorrow. Teenagers often think of the future in terms of something that happens to them rather than something they can shape. Help your kids see that they can have a hand in shaping their own future positively if they set goals based on God's priorities.

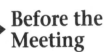

Before the Meeting

You'll need newsprint, markers, tape, pencils and paper. Make sure everyone has a copy of *The Youth Bible*.

1. Timelines

Give each person a sheet of newsprint and a marker.

Say: **The future isn't something that just happens to us. If we take the time to think ahead, with God's help we can mold and shape our lives in positive ways. On your sheet of newsprint, draw a timeline that represents your life from the day you were born to the day you plan to retire. Put dates on the timeline marking the high points you've had and more high points you'd like to see happen in the future.**

Have kids tape the finished timelines to the wall. Allow time for kids to look at others' timelines.

Gather the group together and read aloud the devotion "Assurance of Hope" (p. 630 in *The Youth Bible*).

Say: **Bishop Tutu has a bright spot on his personal timeline. How can he be so confident that he is willing to put it there? How can you have that kind of confidence about your future?**

2. Plotting a Full Future

Form four groups and assign each group one of the following devotions and passages from *The Youth Bible*: "A Hope-Filled Dream," Genesis 9:8-17; "Will Peace Ever Come?" Jeremiah 33:14-16; "The Rock," Matthew 24:36-44; and "Party Now?" 2 Peter 3:8-13.

Say: **Study your group's devotion and passage. Discover at least two things the**

Bible tells us to do if we want to have a full future.

After groups are finished, have them report their answers. As each group reports, write their answers on a sheet of newsprint and tape it to the wall near the timelines. Answers may include helping others, considering the whole world, trusting God and being prepared.

Say: **When we think about our future, it's easy to forget these really important things we just named. The Bible reminds us about God's priorities for our future.**

 3. Taking Control of Your Future

Say: **I want you to go back to your timeline and change it or add to it to reflect these priorities we discovered in the Bible. If your timeline already contains some of the things we listed, you may want to add others. Or you may want to remove things that stand in the way of accomplishing God's priorities for your life.**

When kids have made their timeline adjustments, have them sit in a circle.

 4. Being Prepared

Ask everyone to turn to Mark 13:24-33. Read aloud the passage and the related devotion, "Be Prepared." Lead kids in the first "Consider . . ." suggestion.

Ask: **If you could put only one item in your emergency kit for the end of the**

world, what would it be? What would you put in a kit to take into the future with you?

Go around the circle and let each person tell one thing.

Have kids pair up and look over the "Consider . . ." sections of the devotions they've studied during this session. Have kids each choose one of the suggestions to follow up on and share their choice with their partner. Then bring everyone together and have kids each tell what their partner chose to do.

 5. Wish Upon a Paper

Distribute pencils and paper. Have kids each write their name at the top of their paper.

Say: **Leave your paper at your present place and rotate one spot to the left. Write on the paper in front of you one positive thing you wish for that person's future.**

Have kids continue until they've written on everyone's paper. Then give kids a moment to scan the wishes other people made for them.

Ask: **How does it make you feel to read these wishes?**

Then say: **Your friends can offer you good wishes and help along the way. But your future depends on your own decisions and actions—and on the grace of God. Each of you is your own biographer, and God is your co-author.**

Close with prayer, asking for God's guidance and the ability to recognize his will as kids plan their futures.

GIVING GOD'S WAY

THEME: Giving

Today's kids live in one of the most materialistic societies ever. People are not so much defined by who they are as by what they own—the make of their car, the clothes they wear, the vacations they can afford. Transform your group members' mind-sets to teach them what is really valuable in God's eyes.

▶ Before the Meeting

Set up a cassette or CD player with one of the kids' favorite songs for activity 1. On a table at the front of the room, place three gift-wrapped boxes. In the largest box wrap something kids can share, such as candy or gum. In a smaller box, wrap a non-material gift of self, such as a coupon for a two-minute back rub. Wrap a third box with nothing inside.

Also gather 3×5 cards, stick-on gift bows and an 18-inch length of ribbon for each group member. Make sure you have copies of *The Youth Bible* for everyone.

▶ 1. Give Me, Give Me

When kids arrive, ask them each to tell which gift they would most like to receive and why. Have kids form a line in front of their chosen gift. Then play three rounds of musical chairs—one with each of the three groups—to determine the winners of the three gifts.

Before the three winners open their gifts, ask: **How do you feel when someone gives you a gift? when you give a gift? What things make you feel good about getting a gift?**

Have the three winners open their gifts at once. Give the back rub immediately. Encourage the person who received the gift that could be shared to pass it around so others can help themselves.

Ask the person who received the empty box: **How did you feel when your gift box was empty? What makes us have negative feelings about gifts we receive in real life?**

Say: **Many things influence how we feel about gifts. Today we're going to learn what makes a gift valuable to God.**

2. The Best Gift Ever

Have a volunteer read aloud "Sharing With Joy" (p. 183 in *The Youth Bible*).

Say: **Jennie gave something much more meaningful than a material gift—she gave a gift of herself. What's the most significant "gift of self" you ever received from another person? What's the most significant gift of self you ever gave?**

3. Givers Anonymous

Form two groups. Have each group read one of the following devotions from *The Youth Bible*: "Under Construction" (p. 989) or "The Little Things" (p. 1200). Have kids in each group tell about people they know who are like Stephen and Jennifer and what kind of impact those people have on the lives of others.

4. Giving Wall

Have kids count off by threes to form groups. Give each group one of the following passages from *The Youth B[i...]* Mark 12:38-44; or 2 Co[...] ute 3×5 cards.

Kids in each group will read th[...] discuss the principles of giving it tea[...] have them write those principles on 3×5 c[...] and attach the cards to a wall using stick-on g[...] bows. They may need to add tape to get the cards to stick to the wall.

5. The Gift Goes On

Give kids each a length of ribbon. Then have them pair off. Each pair will look through the "Consider ..." sections of the devotions together. Have partners share plans for giving of themselves this week, then tie ribbons on each other's wrists as a reminder and a commitment to carry out their plans.

Form a circle. Have kids join hands and extend them to the center of the circle. Pray that God will help all the kids become giving people.

MANY-
NDORED
THING

THEME: God's Love

ible: Deuteronomy 26:5-11;
rinthians 8:5-15. Distrib-
i passage and
ches. Then
spards
Then

Teenagers often struggle with harsh, unloving environments and attitudes. Friends, even family members, may reject them as they struggle to find a balance between a need to "break away" and a growing sense of accountability. Kids can take great consolation in the fact that through all the trauma and turmoil of growing up, the love of God is constant and unchanging.

► **Before the Meeting**

Gather pencils, 3×5 cards, large sheets of posterboard or newsprint, tape, markers and a copy of *The Youth Bible* for each group member.

loving act? How do you feel when you hear the Bible's message that God loves you and does loving things for you?

► 1. Love Me Tender

When kids arrive, have them sit in a circle. Give one person a back rub. Then have that person give a back rub to another person while you give one to someone else. Keep the process going until everyone has received a back rub.

Afterward, ask: **How did you feel as you gave a back rub? How did you feel as you received a back rub from someone else? How do you usually feel when someone expresses love to you through words or a**

► 2. Invisible Stuff

While the group is still sitting in a circle, read aloud the devotion "Easy to Take for Granted" (p. 540 in *The Youth Bible*). Pause before revealing that the subject of the article is oxygen and let kids guess what is being described.

Have kids turn to Psalm 103 and ask a volunteer to read it aloud. Then put up a large sheet of newsprint and lead kids in the first "Consider ..." activity.

Say: **We count on God for all these things each day—and he keeps on caring for us whether we take his love for granted or** not. Let's find out some more about how God's love works in our lives.

▶ 3. Non-Stop Love

Form groups of three or more. Assign each group one of the following devotions and passages from *The Youth Bible*: "Persistent Love," Deuteronomy 4:32-40; "You'll Always Be My Baby," Isaiah 66:10-14; "Stubborn Love," Luke 15:1-10; "Shepherds and Sheep," John 10:1-30; "Power to Heal," Acts 3:11-19; "Free Gifts," Romans 11:29-36; "Too Good to Be True?" Galatians 4:4-7; "Tough Times," 2 Thessalonians 2:13—3:5; or "Storm Trackers," Hebrews 4:14—5:10. (You don't need to use all the passages.)

Instruct groups to look for ways God's nonstop love is demonstrated both in the scripture passage and in the devotion. After groups have read through the assigned material and discussed the questions at the end, pull everyone together and have groups share their stories and the encouraging truths they discovered about God's love.

▶ 4. Second-Chance People

Have kids sit in a circle as you read aloud the devotion "A Second Chance" (p. 22 in *The Youth Bible*). Discuss the questions at the end.

Then distribute pencils and 3×5 cards.

Say: **I want yo** you were given a se you "deserved" it or no of the person who gave you chance on your card. Now think one you know who could use a seco chance from you. Write that person's name on the other side of your card.

Have kids tuck their cards in their Bibles. Encourage them to thank God for his love expressed through their "second-chance person" during their devotions this week and also to ask his help in becoming a second-chance person for the other person they listed on the card.

▶ 5. God's Unbelievable Love

Have volunteers read aloud the devotion "Unbelievable" (p. 1220 in *The Youth Bible*) and the accompanying scripture passage, Ephesians 3:14-21. Discuss the questions at the end of the devotion.

Then have kids return to their groups from activity 3. Give each group a sheet of posterboard or newsprint and markers and have them complete the first "Consider ..." activity.

Gather everyone in front of the finished posters. Close with a song such as "Love Carrier" from *The Group Songbook* (Group Books).

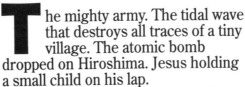

S THE NGEST?

ME: God's Power

> T he mighty army. The tidal wave that destroys all traces of a tiny village. The atomic bomb dropped on Hiroshima. Jesus holding a small child on his lap.
>
> All these are displays of power. Use this meeting to demonstrate to kids that God's power excels all others because his strength expresses itself perfectly in every situation.

Before the Meeting

Gather the power symbols for activity 1: a battery, a toy gun, a dumbbell, a rock, a cross, a match, a crutch and a yearbook. Make sure everyone has a copy of *The Youth Bible*.

1. Power Symbols

Place the power symbols on a table.

Say: **Today we're going to talk about power. Which of these items represents power? What kind of power do these items symbolize to you?**

Allow kids to tell which items symbolize power to them and why. There are no right or wrong answers, so encourage all responses.

Ask: **Do any of these items symbolize weakness to you? Which ones do you feel shouldn't be included in this collection?**

Take a poll by a show of hands, asking: **Which one of these items best symbolizes power? Which one brings to mind the greatest weakness?**

2. Power Games

Form four groups. Assign the groups the following devotions and passages from *The Youth Bible*.

Group 1: "Stronger Than Hatred," Deuteronomy 32:36—33:4; "In Just Fifteen Seconds," Joshua 10:4-14.

Group 2: "Against All Odds," Psalm 40; "The Big Blast," Joel 2:1-2.

Group 3: "The Power of Right," Malachi 3:1-4; "Power in Letting Go," Luke 1:26-38.

Group 4: "Batteries Included," Ephesians 1:15-23; "The World's Strongest Man," Revelation 1:4-18.

Have groups each read their devotions and passages, discuss the questions at the end, and select the symbol from activity 1 that best represents the power demonstrated in their stories.

After 10 minutes, bring everyone back together. Have groups each summarize their devotions and tell why they chose particular power symbols to represent their stories. Again, there are no wrong answers, but possible match-ups may go something like this: "Stronger Than Hatred," cross; "In Just Fifteen Seconds," rock; "Against All Odds," gun; "The Big Blast," match; "The Power of Right," yearbook; "Power in Letting Go," crutch; "Batteries Included," battery; and "The World's Strongest Man," dumbbell.

 ## 3. Power Tools

Say: **As we have just discovered, God's power takes different forms for different situations. God doesn't always blast in, punch through or blow up; sometimes his power appears in ways we might never expect. However God's power is revealed, it's always perfect and adequate for the need at hand.**

Have a volunteer read aloud 2 Corinthians 12:9-10.

Then ask: **When does Paul say God's perfect power is with him? Why do you think this is so? What do these verses suggest we need to do to experience God's power?**

Say: **If we want God's power in our lives we must be willing to confess our weaknesses and our total reliance on him. That's not always easy. There's a side of us that wants to say, "I can do it myself." But surrendering control to God brings marvelous—sometimes miraculous results.**

Ask for volunteers to share times when God demonstrated his power in response to their needs or weaknesses.

▶ 4. Power Play

Say: **Select one of the power symbols from activity 1 that best symbolizes the power needed for a situation you're facing right now.**

Place the power symbols in a large circle. Then have kids go stand by the item that represents a response to their need.

Have kids pray together using sentence prayers. Begin the prayer time by modeling a few of the sentence prayers below. Then allow kids to pray spontaneously, following the models or creating sentence prayers of their own. Avoid going around the circle in order so you don't put pressure on anyone who is uncomfortable praying in this situation.

1. God, we need you to be like a battery, providing us with the power to . . .
2. God, we need you to be like a weight, helping us grow stronger so that . . .
3. God, you are our crutch. As we lean on your power teach us . . .
4. God, we know that you are a weapon of righteousness. We trust you to defeat . . .
5. God, you are our rock! We stand on you in faith for . . .
6. God, we need the flame of your purity and power. Help us burn brightly by . . .
7. God, you record all our deeds in your book. May we so live for you that . . .
8. God, we glory in the power of the cross. May the cross become powerful in our lives by calling us to . . .

Close with a huddle and a pile-on of hands. Have kids break the pile on the count of three, shouting "God's Power!"

NOT MY WILL, BUT YOURS

THEME: God's Will

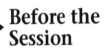

Most of us spend plenty of time thinking about the future and wondering just exactly what God has in mind for us. Teenagers certainly do. Yet we commonly live out only a small portion of what we know God's will to be. This session will help kids see that God's will is continuously revealed as we begin doing the things we know he wants us to do.

Before the Session

Put a "Questions" sign on one wall of your room. Put an "Answers" sign on the opposite wall. Gather pennies, paper, tape, pieces of thread, facial tissues, pencils, 3×5 cards and envelopes.

1. How Do You Figure?

Have kids form groups of three. Give each group the following objects: three pennies, a sheet of paper, a piece of tape, a piece of thread and a facial tissue.

Say: **The first group to do what I want you to do with these objects will be declared the winner. Ready, set, go!**

Kids will be bewildered, because you haven't explained what you want them to do. After a few moments, explain that you'll give some hints.

Say: **Okay, each group can ask me one question, privately. But I will only answer** "yes," "no" or "maybe."

After a few minutes, have groups display the results of their efforts. Ask them to explain how they came up with what they *thought* you wanted.

Say: **No winners! Here's what I wanted you to do: Keep the pennies for extra spending money; make an airplane out of the paper; use the tape to reinforce the airplane; throw away the thread because it's no good without a needle; and give the tissue to anyone in the group with a runny nose.**

Then ask: **How did it feel trying to figure out what I wanted when I gave you so little direction? Was it fair? How is this like trying to figure out God's will for your life? How clearly does God let us know his will? Do you ever feel God isn't fair because it's sometimes so hard to figure out what he wants us to do?**

2. God's Puzzlers

Break into groups of no more than four. Assign each group one of the following devotions from *The Youth Bible*: "Unknown Outcomes" (p. 14), "Following the Guidelines" (p. 79), "God's Surprises" (p. 911) or "A Life Pleasing God" (p. 1238).

Say: **Sometimes God leads us through puzzling or even disappointing circumstances. As you read your devotions, identify those circumstances. Discuss how you would have felt and reacted.**

After a few minutes, call the groups together and have them share the stories they studied.

Ask: **Does God work in our lives even when seemingly bad things happen? How do these stories make that point?**

 ## 3. Follow Your Heart

Assign each group one of the following devotions: "Against the Grain" (p. 1010), "Daring to Follow" (p. 1051), "Close to Your Heart" (p. 1123) or "Mother Hale" (p. 1140).

Say: **As you read these stories, think about what made these people tick. What problems or opposition did they face? How did they know that following this course of action was truly God's will?**

Again, pull groups together and have them share what they discovered.

Ask: **What do these stories have in common?**

4. Questions and Answers

Have kids return to their groups and read the scriptures that accompany their devotions.

Distribute pencils and 3×5 cards.

Say: **I want you to look for the principles these Bible passages teach about following God's will. Write them down on 3×5 cards and tape them up on the Answers wall.**

You may still have lots of questions about finding and following God's will. Write them down on 3×5 cards, and tape them up to the Questions wall. I'd like each person to write at least one question and one answer.

After several minutes, pull the groups together. Review the answers, then the questions. Challenge kids to try matching the principles on the Answers wall with some of the questions on the Questions wall.

Say: **There are times we all wish God would send us a blueprint or a checklist that would help us understand what's going on in our lives. But our human minds can never fully comprehend God's wisdom. That's where trust enters the picture.**

5. God Can Handle It

Have a volunteer read aloud James 4:13-17 in *The Youth Bible* and the accompanying devotion "Lump on an All-Star's Arm." Then discuss the questions that follow the devotion.

Hand out envelopes and lead kids in the second "Consider . . . " exercise.

Close by singing a song of trust, such as "In His Time."

GETTING INTO THE LAW

THEME: Government

Even though the voting age is 18, kids still tend to think of government as something far removed from their lives. Government is something that does things to us—it makes laws, levies taxes and gives speeding tickets. This meeting encourages kids to break out of the passive mode and observe government first hand. They'll see not only how they fit into government structure, but also how God does.

Before the Meeting

Activity 1 lists several ways your kids can experience the workings of government firsthand. Some can be done on weekdays or week nights, others can be done on weekends. Choose one and do it as a group. After the activity, return to the church to complete the meeting.

Gather newsprint, markers, several recent copies of your local newspaper, and a copy of *The Youth Bible* for each group member.

1. A Piece of the Action

Choose one of these activities to do as a group prior to your meeting:

- Visit a criminal court and watch a trial in progress.
- Visit a city council meeting.
- Visit a school board meeting.
- Visit the local office of your senator or congressional representative.

- Invite a school board member, a city council person or other local politician who is a Christian to speak to your group. Ask them to explain how their religious faith has affected their political work.

2. Back on the Home Front

After the experience is over, bring everyone together and ask: **What sticks out in your mind about this experience? Did you feel nervous? What other emotions did you experience?**

Go around the room and have kids each complete this statement: From this experience, I would say that government is ...

Say: **Government isn't always glamorous, ethical or fair. But it does fulfill a vital role in maintaining order in our nation. Let's take a look at a couple of devotions and scriptures that give us further insight into government.**

3. Respectfully Yours

Form three groups. Assign each group one of the following passages: Romans 13:1-10; Colossians 1:15-17 or 1 Timothy 2:1-6.

Say: **Your task is to discover in your passage at least two principles about rulers and government. You'll have three minutes to read and discuss your passage. Go!**

After three minutes, call time and have groups report. Jot down on newsprint the principles they share.

Then say: **Keeping these principles in mind, I want you to imagine yourself in the middle of the situation I'm about to explain. To prepare yourselves for this experience, please scatter around the classroom, find a place by yourself, sit down on the floor and close your eyes.**

When kids are in place, read this story.

After tonight's meeting, you go home to find your house empty and dark. You call out, but no one answers. You sense something is wrong. You flick on the lights. A scene of devastation and destruction appears before you. Pictures, vases and lamps have been smashed; sofas and chairs slashed; and hateful slogans spray-painted on the walls. You run up to your room. Your stereo is missing and the contents of your dresser are scattered across the floor. You dash back down to the kitchen. Dishes and glasses lie in a thousand pieces. Your dog is lying very still on the floor.

Suddenly you hear a noise outside. You dart behind the refrigerator. Your neighbor calls out your name softly. You step out of your hiding place. Your neighbor grabs you and says in a trembling voice, "I'm so sorry! The police did this. They took your parents and little Ben away. Oh—I'm so sorry!"

After a moment of silence, tell kids to open their eyes but stay in their places on the floor.

Ask: **How did you feel as you put yourself in this situation? Could something like this** ever really happen?

Refer to the scriptural principles you listed on newsprint.

Ask: **Keeping these principles in mind, what is an appropriate Christian response to this kind of tyranny? Do you think governments that unjustly persecute people are truly ordained by God? How have Christians and Jews historically responded to persecution? How would you, personally, respond?**

Say: **It's not always easy to understand God's purposes in history and in world events. But we do know that these scriptures about Christian response to authority were written in a time of great persecution. We also know that God communicated his expectations to leaders as well as to common people. Let's see what the Bible has to say to and about those in authority.**

 4. Rulers as Servants

Form two groups, and assign each group one of the following devotions from *The Youth Bible*: "Respected Leaders" and "An Inch Is as Good as a Mile." Have groups read their devotions and discuss the questions at the end.

Bring everyone together and ask: **What did your devotion teach about Christian leadership?**

Have a volunteer read 2 Samuel 23:1-5 aloud.

Then ask: **Can you think of a leader— either current or historical—who fits this description? What would it be like to live under the leadership of a person like this? Did you see any Christian leadership in our government experience? Do you think Christians should be more active in seeking public office? Explain.**

5. Action Issues

Distribute several recent copies of your local newspaper. Have kids search through them and clip articles on local government issues. Give kids an opportunity to share their articles, then take a vote on which issue they'd like to try to influence by their involvement.

Say: **From this point on we're a political action team. Let's brainstorm ways we can have a positive influence in this situation.**

Record kids' ideas on a sheet of newsprint. Examples might include: writing letters to government officials, writing letters to the newspaper, preparing and distributing informative fliers on the issue, picketing, contacting other youth groups to create a larger base of support, and contacting local media. Have kids vote on which action to take. If your group is larger, you might divide into two or three action teams with different responsibilities.

Once kids have decided on a plan of action, designate people for specific responsibilities, schedule dates and deadlines, and allow time for kids to get started on their projects.

When it's time to bring the work session to a close, say: **As Christians in a democracy, there are endless options for influencing the way government operates. But the most powerful tool we have to effect change in government is prayer.**

▶ **6. Prayer for Leaders**

Close with a circle of prayer. Ask group members to pray for God's guidance and protection in this effort, for pure motives, for people to see Christ's love reflected, for group members with specific responsibilities, and for government leaders involved.

DON'T WORRY, BE...YOU KNOW!

THEME: Happiness

> **P**ain serves the beneficial purpose of telling us when something is wrong, when our bodies need to be rested or repaired. Pain pills give back the message, "Okay! I know I'm injured. You don't have to shout!"
>
> How often have you wished for a pain pill to ease life's hurts for yourself or the kids in your group? There is no simple medication that provides instant happiness, but we can learn to dispense words of hope and truth capable of easing the worst case of despair.

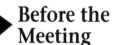

Before the Meeting

Blow up a balloon and draw a sad face on it. Gather newsprint, a marker, small jars, labels, small candies, paper, pencils and sandwich bags. Make sure you have a copy of *The Youth Bible* for each group member.

1. Happy Camper

Hold the sad-face balloon in your hand.

Say: **I need volunteers for a project that requires some sensitivity.**

Recruit three volunteers without explaining the exact nature of their task. Line them up in front of the other kids.

Then hold up the balloon and say to the volunteers: **Your job is to try to cheer up our poor, unhappy friend.**

Encourage the volunteers to put their hearts into the project.

After a few minutes of balloon therapy, ask:

How did you feel trying to cheer up this balloon? How did it feel watching these kids trying to cheer up our unhappy balloon? How is trying to cheer up this balloon like trying to cheer up someone who's really discouraged or depressed? What usually helps you break out of a cycle of unhappiness?

Say: **Let's look in the Bible and try to discover the way to true happiness in life.**

2. Case Histories

Form five groups. (A group can be as small as one person.) Assign each group two of the following devotions and passages from *The Youth Bible*: "In the Here and Now," Ecclesiastes 2:18-26; "Glad You're Here ... Finally," Zephaniah 3:14-18; "The Secret of Real Happiness," Matthew 5:1-12; "Real Treasure," Matthew 13:44-52; and "The Hope Giver," 1 Peter 1:3-9.

Say: **As you read through your devotions,**

think of yourselves as doctors and the characters in the stories as patients. Be prepared to share their "case histories" with the rest of the group.

Have groups read their passages and devotions and discuss the questions at the end. Then bring everyone together and have groups share their case histories.

After each group's presentation, ask: **If the scripture passages you read could be put into pill form, what would they do to help the patient achieve happiness? What would you call these medicines?** (Possible "medicines" might include thankfulness, friendship, purpose, simplicity, integrity and salvation.) List the medicines named by the groups on a sheet of newsprint.

Have groups each make labels with the names of their medicines and the scripture reference, put the labels on glass jars, and fill the jars with candy. The "pharmacy" will grow as groups continue to present their case histories and name the medicines for happiness they find in their scripture passages.

▶ 3. Personal Happiness

Have kids turn to Psalm 23. Ask volunteers to read Psalm 23 and the devotion "Heart Strokes" aloud.

Distribute paper and pencils and lead kids in the first "Consider ..." activity, encouraging each person to write several endings to the sentence "Happiness, for me, is ... "

Have kids share their responses.

Ask: **What medicine could we add to our pharmacy from Psalm 23?** (Peace would be an appropriate medicine.) Have volunteers label another bottle, fill it with candy and add the new medicine to the others.

▶ 4. Boomerang Happiness

Have kids turn to "Creating Happiness" (p. 1248 in *The Youth Bible*). Ask volunteers to read aloud the devotion and the related scripture passage, 1 Thessalonians 3:9-13. Have kids create a medicine from this passage, as well. (A possibility is ministry.)

Then say: **Now turn your papers over and think about your "dark valleys." Write down the last time you were really *un*happy. What happened? Is there something in your life that makes you consistently unhappy?**

Allow time for sharing.

Say: **We created this wonderful pharmacy full of medicine from the Bible that will help us react to our unhappy situations in the positive way Juanita did. Which of these medicines would help most with your unhappy situation? Step right up and help yourself.**

▶ 5. Portable Clinic

Distribute sandwich bags and labels.

Say: **The interesting thing about happiness is that it most often comes to us when we're trying to give it away. Think of someone you know who's been unhappy lately. Write a prescription for some of our biblical medicine on the label, along with an encouraging scripture passage. Then make it a point to see that person this week and give the medicine along with a hug!**

Encourage kids to look in the "For More, See ..." sections of the devotions they read to find appropriate passages for their labels. Have them fill the sandwich bags with candy from the jars in the pharmacy.

Close with prayer, asking God's blessing and true happiness on the lives of each person present, and on the people kids will reach out to during the week.

CALLING ALL HEROES

THEME: Heroes

Families come unglued. Sports figures die from drug overdoses. Media stars flaunt open sexual relationships. No wonder kids today don't know who to follow as a hero. Many teenagers select inappropriate or misguided heroes. Help your kids discover the characteristics of a true hero. This session will help them decide how to select personal heroes and how to keep their admiration within appropriate bounds.

▶ Before the Meeting

Gather newspapers or news magazines, newsprint, a marker, envelopes and pens. If it's possible, obtain a cassette of "Wind Beneath My Wings" by Bette Midler and a cassette player. Photocopy the "Certificate for a Hero" handout. Provide soft drinks and the ingredients for hero sandwiches. Make sure everyone has a copy of *The Youth Bible*.

▶ 1. I Need A Hero

Hand out newspapers or news magazines. Tell kids to tear out headlines and photo features about today's heroes. Let them share their findings.

Ask: **What does the world want in a hero?**

Write their comments on a sheet of newsprint.

Ask: **What are some dangers of choosing a hero based on the world's standards?**

▶ 2. The One True Hero

Form two groups.

Say: **The Bible has a different point of view about heroes. Let's look at the characteristics of biblical heroes.**

Assign one group the devotion "Risky Business" from *The Youth Bible* and the related scripture, Esther 4:9-16. Assign the other group the devotion "Admire, Don't Worship" and the related scripture, Acts 14:8-18. Give each group newsprint and markers.

Say: **Identify the main hero in the scripture. On the newsprint sketch each hero in action using stick figures and brief captions.**

Bring kids together and call on each group to share its sketches.

Ask: **Who is the one common hero in all**

of these stories? What characteristics of God make him the one true hero? How are the characters in the devotions like or unlike God, the true hero? How is it helpful to have a personal hero?

 ## 3. Hero Selection

Ask the second Bible study question from "Risky Business" and "Admire, Don't Worship."

Ask volunteers to look up the verses from the "For More, See ..." section in "How Hard They Fall" (p. 1167 in *The Youth Bible*) and read them aloud. Have another person read aloud 1 Corinthians 1:1-17.

Ask: **What advice can you find in these verses about how to select and evaluate a hero?**

As kids call out advice from these verses, record it on newsprint. Compare this list to the world's list of a hero's characteristics from activity 1.

 ## 4. You Are My Hero

Say: **Heroes don't have to be famous people.**

If you were able to obtain a cassette of "Wind Beneath My Wings," play it now. Then discuss the characteristics of this person's hero. Compare this hero to the worldly and biblical lists of heroes' characteristics kids compiled earlier.

Give kids each a "Certificate for a Hero" handout.

Say: **Think of someone who has been a hero to you. This can be a relative, someone in your church or school, or a friend. Complete this certificate by identifying the qualities that you admire about this hero and checking off ways this person has guided you.**

Allow a few minutes for kids to work. Then call on volunteers to share their heroes. Pass out envelopes.

Say: **Address this envelope to your hero. If you don't know the address, write the hero's name on the envelope and complete the rest of the address later. Be sure to drop these in the mail tomorrow.**

 ## 5. Hero Fellowship

Form groups of three or four. Have kids in each group pray for their heroes by name. Ask them also to pray that God will reveal other healthy role models for them.

Lay out ingredients for hero sandwiches (you may call them "subs" or "hoagies"). Have kids help put the sandwiches together. Serve soft drinks with the sandwiches. As kids eat, lead them in the second "Consider ..." suggestion from "How Hard They Fall" (p. 1167 in *The Youth Bible*). Between bites, have kids tell why only Jesus can be a perfect hero.

CERTIFICATE FOR A HERO

Whereas this person has modeled these qualities:

_____

_____

_____ ;

Whereas this person has provided:
(check the appropriate boxes)

- ❏ encouragement
- ❏ concern
- ❏ a caring heart
- ❏ unconditional love
- ❏ opportunities to grow
- ❏ personal challenges
- ❏ a listening ear
- ❏ support;

Let it be known this _____ day of the month of

_____

in the year of _____, that

_____

(hero's name)

is a certified genuine hero in the life of

_____

(your name)

With warmest thanks and appreciation.

HOLY *WHO?*

THEME: The Holy Spirit

Sometimes it may seem that God is off in some unreachable spiritual dimension. Yet, the amazing message of the Bible is that our almighty God lives within us—in the person of the Holy Spirit. He indwells us and steers us through periods of temptation, helping us make good choices. This meeting will help kids become aware of how much the Holy Spirit is involved in their lives.

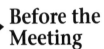

Before the Meeting

Gather several of 6-foot lengths of yarn (not string—it needs to be breakable), an 8-foot 2×4, newsprint, markers, 3×5 cards, pencils and a magnifying glass. Also make sure you have a copy of *The Youth Bible* for everyone.

1. The Straight and Narrow

Have kids form groups of three. Place the 2×4 in the center of the floor. Explain that you'll be playing several rounds of a game called Walking the Straight and Narrow. Each group will have one walker and two tempters. The walker will hold a 6-foot length of yarn in each hand. The tempters will hold the other ends. As the walker tries to walk down the 2×4, the tempters will yank on the yarn, trying to throw the walker off balance.

The rules are: The walker may not let go of the yarn; the tempters may not touch the walker; if the yarn breaks, the walker automatically wins; and the walker will be disqualified for touching the floor.

Have groups play three rounds so each person can have a turn being the walker.

After everyone has played, ask: **How did you feel being pulled in two directions at once? How was this activity like trying to get through a day without giving in to temptation? What is the source of your ability to detect and resist temptation?**

2. A Day in the Life

Ask for a volunteer scribe. Have kids come up with a typical day's schedule, including times and activities. The scribe will record the schedule on a large sheet of newsprint. Then have the scribe sit down.

Hand the marker to someone and say: **Insert an arrow into the schedule when teenagers might typically face some kind of tempta-**

tion. **Label the arrow with the temptation that might occur.**

Have the person who inserts a temptation hand the marker to someone else who will insert another temptation. Keep the process going until everyone has had a chance to insert a temptation.

Ask: **How does looking at this list make you feel? How can you handle all these temptations?**

Say: **If you're a Christian, the conflict you feel with temptation is the influence of the Holy Spirit in your life—urging you to stay within the safe guidelines God has established. According to the promise of Jesus, the Holy Spirit is with us, influencing us for the good. Let's find out more from the Bible.**

3. Mix and Match

Have kids turn to "The Improbable Disciple" (p. 1087 in *The Youth Bible*). Ask volunteers to read aloud the devotion and related passage, John 16:4-15.

Ask: **How does the Holy Spirit work to bring about change in a person's life? When have you felt the Holy Spirit work to change you?**

Lead kids in the first "Consider ..." idea. Form two groups. Give each group 10 3×5 cards and a pencil. Have one group think up 10 alternatives for the word "Holy" as the other group thinks up 10 alternatives for the word "Spirit." Then gather everyone together and mix and match the words to form new combinations that show how the Holy Spirit works in our lives. Encourage kids to maintain a serious, respectful attitude even if some of the combinations sound unusual or humorous.

Say: **The Holy Spirit works in our lives in all these ways—the key thing for us is to be sensitive to his presence.**

▶ 4. On Track

Have kids turn to Acts 2:1-21. Read aloud the passage and the related devotion, "The Third Rail."

Ask: **How does the Holy Spirit give power to Christians? What indicates that the Holy Spirit has empowered someone? What is your own experience with the work of the Holy Spirit?**

▶ 5. The Evidence

Have kids sit in a circle. Hold a magnifying glass.

Say: **Think back over the last week. What evidence can you find that the Holy Spirit was working in your life?**

Pass around the magnifying glass. As kids hold it, have them share their evidence or tell how they're going to try to respond to the Holy Spirit's presence and teaching.

Close the class with prayer, thanking God for these specific instances of the Holy Spirit's guidance.

STILL THE BEST POLICY?

THEME: Honesty

Honesty is the best policy. We occasionally wonder if this old line really works for us today. We look at our world and realize that it is often *dis*honesty that gets people ahead. Are we suckers and losers for playing it straight? What does God have to say to us about it? This meeting will help kids consider the biblical view of honesty and how it relates to personal success and failure.

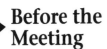

Before the Meeting

Secretly arrange for two kids in your group to play the role of cheater in the "Play to Win!" activity. Explain that they should cheat in any way possible and encourage other kids to cheat too.

Write two sets of clues for the game on 3×5 cards. Also gather newsprint, markers, prizes, a small bell, paper slips, pencils, matches and a metal waste container that can safely hold a small fire. Make sure everyone has a copy of *The Youth Bible*.

1. Play to Win!

Form two teams. Secretly plant a cheater on each team. Explain that you'll be playing a modified version of Pictionary with all the clues centering around the theme of honesty. Give each team a pad of newsprint and a marker. Show the prize you've brought for the winning team and make it look really desirable to win the game.

At the sound of the bell, one member of each team runs to the front of the room for a clue card. (Give the same clue to both teams.) Those team members run back to their own teams and draw pictures to represent the clue. The "artist" may not use letters and may not speak.

The first team to guess correctly wins that round. In the next round, two more team members retrieve the clue and draw it.

Here are some possible clues:
● A little white lie
● Honesty is the best policy
● Satan
● Truth or Dare
● A cover-up
● George Washington
● The whole truth and nothing but the truth
● Lie like a rug

After the game, explain that the cheaters were planted on each team.

Ask: **What was your initial reaction when you discovered that some kids were cheat-**

ing? In what ways did that make it easier for you to cheat? How did it feel to "get ahead" by cheating? How can competition encourage dishonesty?

Say: **Sometimes we may feel angry when we discover others getting ahead through dishonesty. We may be tempted to do the same. During this meeting we will explore some Christian principles and guidelines for honesty.**

▶ 2. On the Slide of Truth

Form five groups (a group can be as small as one person). Give each group newsprint and a marker and assign one of the following devotions and passages from *The Youth Bible*: "Truth and Consequences," Genesis 26:1-11; "The Cover-Up," Leviticus 19:1-18; "Slow, But Sure," Psalm 112; "Slow to Heal," Jeremiah 23:23-30; or "The Whole Truth," Ezekiel 3:16-21.

Say: **As you read through your devotion and passage, think about what they teach you about honesty. Write at least two principles about honesty on your newsprint.**

Allow time for study and discussion. Then bring everyone together and have groups report their findings.

After all groups have reported, ask: **In your opinion, what is the most compelling reason to be dishonest? to be honest? How hard is it for teenagers today to be consistently honest? Explain. What would be your advice to a teenager who's considering lying to avoid getting in trouble?**

▶ 3. Rumor Mill

Have kids turn to Acts 6:8-15 in *The Youth Bible*. Ask a volunteer to read the passage aloud. Ask another volunteer to read aloud the related devotion, "Rumors."

Discuss the questions at the end of the Bible study. Then have kids return to the groups from activity 1. Have each group do one of the "Consider ..." activities. Then bring the groups together and have them share their ideas.

▶ 4. Forgiveness Fire

Distribute a small slip of paper (about 2 inches square) and a pencil to each group member. Ask kids each to write down an instance during the last week, month or year when they were dishonest. Assure them that no one will see or read these papers.

After kids have written their confessions, have them fold their papers in half and hold on to them.

Have the group form a circle. Invite kids each to pray silently for forgiveness then drop their paper into a metal waste container that's being passed around the circle.

When the prayer circle is completed, have kids follow you as you carry the waste container outside to an open area. Set the paper slips on fire. Talk about how God's love burns away our sins of dishonesty when we ask for forgiveness.

Close with a reading of 1 John 1:9.

CARING FOR THE LEAST OF THESE

THEME: Hunger and Poverty

> **T**he poor will always be with you. Anything you did for any of my people here, you also did for me.
> Jesus made both these statements. They remind us that issues of hunger and poverty won't go away, and that responsible Christians need to address the needs of suffering people of the world.

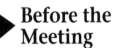

Before the Meeting

Gather masking tape, newsprint and a marker. Wrap a loaf of french bread in a large napkin and set it aside. Get a copy of *The Youth Bible* for each student.

1. Not Fair

Ask for five volunteers to be in a race. Mark start and finish lines on the floor with masking tape.

Say: **Before we start the race, I need to explain a few conditions.**

Assign handicaps to four of the participants. Include hopping on one leg, walking backwards, crab walking, and saying "I've never felt so silly" between every step. The fifth participant will remain handicap-free.

Run the race.

Then ask the participants: **How did you feel when I explained the conditions of the race? How are those feelings like the feel-**ings of people who live in poverty?

Ask the kids who watched the race: **How did you feel watching this competition? How do those feelings compare to being a well-fed person in a hungry world?**

Have a volunteer read aloud the devotion "The Numbers Tell the Story" (p. 564 in *The Youth Bible*).

Say: **Life isn't fair. Some people live in circumstances that don't seem right to anybody. Poverty and hunger hurt millions of people in every country on our planet. What's a Christian to do?**

2. Attitudes and Actions

Form four groups (a group can be one person). Assign one of the following devotions and passages from *The Youth Bible* to each group: "Letting God Use You," 1 Kings 17:8-16; "A Blanket of Love," Nehemiah 5:1-11; "One Friend at a Time," Psalm 72; or "The Multiplication Principle," Mark 6:30-44.

Have groups each examine their devotion and passage and answer the questions at the end. Then bring everyone together and have a spokesperson from each group tell what positive attitudes and actions their character demonstrated toward people in need.

▶ 3. Lay Your Burden Down

Say: **I need the help of a strong and willing volunteer.**

Have the volunteer stand beside you. Start loading down the volunteer with various items from the room, such as a chair, a couple of books, a purse and a box of facial tissues. Don't be afraid to get a little crazy.

When your volunteer is almost to the point of overload, say: **It wouldn't be polite to leave our volunteer suffering like this. Suppose just one of you wanted to help by taking the volunteer's place. Would that be a good way to deal with the problem? Explain. What could we do to spread the burden out a bit?**

Encourage several of the kids to help the volunteer by each taking an item and holding it. When the burden has been distributed among all the kids, have them all "lay their burdens down."

Then ask the volunteer: **How did you feel while you were buried under all that stuff? How did you feel as the burden on you was being reduced? How are your feelings like the feelings of those who bear the burdens of hunger and poverty?**

Ask the others: **How did the rest of you feel watching the volunteer struggle? How did you feel about finally doing something to help? How are those feelings like what you experience when you take action to help those who live in hunger and poverty?**

▶ 4. Doers!

Say: **There are things we can do to help people in need. You can all be God's agents to help make a difference in their lives. Let's talk about things we can do as individuals, and as a group, to help people in need.**

Record kids' responses on newsprint with a marker. Encourage them to refer to the "Consider . . ." sections of the devotions from activities 1 and 2 for ideas.

Vote on one of the ideas to adopt as a group project. Set up goals, deadlines and project coordinators.

▶ 5. One Loaf, One World

Have kids stand in a circle around a table. Place a loaf of french bread in the center of the table. Encourage kids to step forward in silence and break off a piece of bread.

As they hold their piece of bread, say a prayer acknowledging God as the source of all our blessings, and asking his help in sharing those blessings with people in need. Then have kids each feed their piece of bread to a person standing to the right of them as a symbol of their commitment to be faithful to the world's hungry people.

WILL THE REAL CHRISTIAN PLEEEZE STAND UP?

THEME: Hypocrisy

A lmost more than anything else, kids want to feel accepted and loved. They can find the acceptance they're longing for through a relationship with Christ but often look to people instead. People-pleasers tend to wear different "faces" to match their current crowd. This leads to kids forgetting who they really are and losing their sense of value and self-worth. This meeting helps kids see through the traps of hypocrisy and find the strength to live with integrity.

Before the Meeting

Gather newsprint, markers, tape, and a dictionary. Make sure you have a copy of *The Youth Bible* for each person.

1. Pick Your Ending

As kids arrive, form four groups. Assign each group one of the following devotions from *The Youth Bible*: "Are You for Real?" (p. 677), "Empty Words" (p. 846), "Sunday Christians" (p. 946), or "Being an Example" (p. 949). Explain that each group is to read its devotion, then create two dramas based on it—one telling the story just as it's written and the other with an alternative ending.

When groups are ready, have them present their dramas. After each group performs, have kids vote on which of the two dramas they thought was the authentic ending and which

was made up by the group. For fun, take a foot count instead of a hand count when kids vote.

After all the teams have performed, ask: **Do you like acting? Why or why not? What was fun about re-creating the endings to these stories? What was hard about it? How is acting like being a hypocrite? How is making up new endings like what hypocrites do?**

Say: **Pretending to be something you're not can be fun in the right context, but it can also become a dangerous crutch. Today we're going to look at hypocrisy and its consequences.**

2. Hypocrisy Defined

Tape a sheet of newsprint to the wall and write the word "Hypocrite" in large letters along the top. Have kids say what they think hypocrite means. Write their responses on the newsprint. Then have a volunteer read aloud the dictionary definition of the word. Compare the dictionary definition with kids' responses.

Say: **Hypocrisy is a big issue. Let's discover what the Bible says about it.**

Have kids return to the four groups. Assign each group the scripture passage that relates to the devotion they read earlier. Passages include: Isaiah 58:3-9a; Amos 5:18-24; Matthew 21:28-32; and Matthew 23:1-12.

Say: **As you read through your passage, decide what it teaches about hypocrisy that we could add to our definition. Also look for ways hypocrisy is expressed and what kinds of consequences result.**

After kids have studied and discussed their passages, bring everyone together and have groups share their findings.

Ask: **In what ways do Christian kids today struggle with hypocrisy? How do these passages address today's struggles?**

Say: **All of us bump into hypocrisy. Sometimes it's our problem, but sometimes we find ourselves bearing the brunt of another person's hypocrisy. Let's look more closely at what that's like and how we can respond.**

▶ 3. Open Letter to God

Read aloud the devotion "An Open Letter to God" (p. 976 in *The Youth Bible*).

Ask: **What was hypocritical about what Craig's dad did? How could Craig appropriately express his feelings to his dad?**

Next, read aloud the related scripture passage, Mark 7:1-23.

Tape a sheet of newsprint to the wall. At the top, write "Dear Craig," and at the bottom, write "Love, God."

Say: **Considering the scripture we have studied today, how do you think God might encourage Craig in this situation?**

Write kids' comments on the newsprint.

Say: **Hypocrisy can be overcome when we look to God for help and apply ourselves to being "real" with others.**

▶ 4. Get Real

Form groups of three. Have kids each recall one time this month when they felt the brunt of another person's hypocrisy. The other group members will work together to suggest a healthy way to respond to that type of hypocrisy.

When each person has shared, repeat the process, this time asking kids to recall one time this month when they acted hypocritically. The other kids in the group will brainstorm ways to resist acting hypocritically in those situations.

Say: **Forgiving another person's hypocrisy is easier when we see how hypocrisy can infiltrate our own lives. By sticking together as God's family, we can encourage each other to "be real" in the midst of a world full of masks.**

Close the session by having kids pray together in their groups of three, asking God's help for each other to be genuine, honest and loving in the situations where it's most difficult.

"IF ONLY I COULD BE LIKE…"

THEME: Jealousy

Today's emphasis on things and appearance enhances an already natural urge to be jealous of people who have more or look better than we do. And no one is more susceptible to the urge of the green jealousy monster than teenagers. Use this session to help your kids see the futility of jealousy and the joy we can have in knowing that God takes care of us.

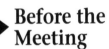

▶ Before the Meeting

Gather newsprint, a marker, a dollar bill, a crayon, old magazines, posterboard, paper and pencils. Hide a supply of markers outside the room for activity 4. Make sure you have a copy of *The Youth Bible* for each person.

▶ 1. Perfectly Jealous

Ask: **What makes the perfect person?**

Have kids list the "perfect" traits of the most perfect person in their school. List the traits on newsprint.

After developing a long list, ask: **How do you feel toward that person? Does jealousy ever keep you from being nice to someone who seems better than you in some way? Have you ever done anything to purposely make someone jealous of you?**

Say: **It's easy to get jealous. We can usually find someone who has more money,** ability or good looks than we do. But getting jealous doesn't help anyone. We're going to take a look at jealousy today.

▶ 2. Dangling Dollar

Pull out a dollar bill and dangle it in front of your class.

Say: **The first person who can come up and take this from my hand can have it.**

Stop talking and continue dangling the dollar bill. When someone takes it, let him or her have it.

Say: **See, that was easy. The dollar is all yours.**

After kids stop booing, ask: **How do you feel toward the person who got the money? Did you have a chance to get the money? Is your jealousy justified? Is jealousy ever okay?**

Say: **We're going to take a look at some**

examples of jealousy in the Bible and see what resulted from it.

3. Jealousy Exposed

Form two groups. Give each group a sheet of newsprint. Be sure there are no extra markers in the room. Give one group a nice marker and give the other a stubby crayon. If kids question it, just tell them you don't have any more markers available.

Assign one group the devotion "A Door to Greater Evil" (p. 1119 in *The Youth Bible*) and the related scripture passage, Acts 13:44-52. Assign the other group the devotion "When Others Succeed" and the related scripture passage, Luke 22:24-30. Have groups each read their story and passage and list on their newsprint these three things: Who was jealous? What did they do? What happened as a result?

When kids are finished, call groups together and have them report on what they found.

Then ask: **How did you in the group with the crayon feel when the other group had a marker? Were the other group's answers better because they had a marker? Explain. What makes jealousy pop up like that? How would the people in the stories and the Bible have been better off if they hadn't gotten jealous?**

4. Genuine Jealousy

Say: **It's easy to get jealous about all kinds of things. Let's take a look at things teenagers get jealous about today.**

Brainstorm things your kids see other teenagers get jealous about. List the ideas on newsprint. When you've got a long list, have kids vote to choose the top five jealousy-causers. Form five groups. If you have fewer than 10 kids, choose fewer jealousy-causers and form fewer groups so that you have at least two kids per group.

Assign each group one of the top five jealousy-causers and have each group develop and pre-

sent a way to combat jealousy in that area. They can choose to make a poster with the old magazines, posterboard and markers; write and perform a song based on a familiar tune; or do a skit depicting someone avoiding jealousy. Make art supplies available, including the markers you hid earlier.

Give kids about ten minutes to prepare; then have them make their presentations.

5. Trumped

Say: **Let's take a look at one more modern example of why people get jealous.**

Have kids read the devotion "The Donald" (p. 503 in *The Youth Bible*).

Ask: **Was it wise to have been jealous of Donald Trump? Explain.**

Have kids read through Psalm 37 silently.

Say: **When you come across a verse that applies to someone like Donald Trump, read that verse aloud.**

When kids have gotten through the whole passage, say: **I'll bet every one of us can think of someone we're jealous of. Think about that person right now. Why are you jealous of that person? Does God love that person any more than he does you? Does God love that person any less than he loves you?**

6. Our Creator's Care

Say: **God created us and loves us. We've got no good reason to be jealous of anyone else. He provides for our needs and takes care of us.**

Read aloud Psalm 37:39-40.

Say: **Why should we be jealous of anyone else when we've got the Creator of the universe looking out for us?**

Close by having kids pray sentence prayers. Encourage kids to pray specific prayers asking God to help them avoid jealousy in areas that are particularly troublesome.

REFLECTING THE SON

THEME: Jesus Christ

Dark hair ... piercing eyes ... a faraway look ... a radiant expression—how do kids see Jesus Christ? And how does his life affect theirs? Challenge kids to know Jesus personally and to discover the features in his life they want to imitate.

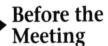

Before the Meeting

Gather newsprint, markers, a few newspapers, pencils and 3×5 cards. You will also need a copy of *The Youth Bible* for each student.

1. A Picture in Words

Write "Jesus" at the top of a large sheet of newsprint and put it up on the wall. Distribute markers.

Say: **We're going to create a word-picture of Jesus. I want each of you to write two or three words or phrases that describe who Jesus is.**

Encourage kids to write expressively, in styles that convey the meaning of the words.

Have kids stand back and admire the "portrait."

Ask: **How did you feel trying to create this portrait of Jesus? What surprises you about the portrait? What qualities of Jesus** are most important to you personally?

Say: **During this meeting, we'll explore who Jesus is and how we can reflect his image in our lives.**

2. A Personal Glimpse

Form three groups. Assign each group one of the following devotions from *The Youth Bible*: "What Love Looks Like," Isaiah 52:13—53:12; "Unexpected Savior," Mark 15:33-39; or "Point to the Light," John 1:1-18.

After reading the devotion and passage and answering the questions, have kids each tell about a person they've known who really showed them what Christ was like.

3. Supporting Evidence

Divide into two groups. Give each group one or two newspapers. Have one group find evidence in the newspaper that Jesus Christ is alive and well in today's society. Have the other group look for evidence supporting the view that Jesus Christ is dead. Call time after five minutes and ask each group to present its evidence.

Ask: **How did you feel as you searched for articles to support your group's point of view? Do the results present a convincing argument? How does the society we live in affect our faith? Did this search make you feel like taking some sort of action? Explain.**

4. A Day With Jesus

Have kids find partners.

Say: **I want you to review how you spent your day yesterday with your partner. Tell what you did, where you went, what kind of mood you were in and how you interacted with people. After you have each spoken, go through your day again, this time imagining Jesus by your side.**

Tell what you would have done differently.

After kids have shared, bring the group together.

Ask: **How did it feel to walk through your day with Jesus? What did you learn about yourself?**

5. In His Image

Have a volunteer read Philippians 2:5-11 aloud. Distribute 3×5 cards and pencils.

Say: **Write "Jesus" on one side of your card. On the other side, write the qualities of Jesus you would like to reflect in your life.**

Suggest that kids take their cards home and tape them to a mirror as a reminder to develop those qualities and reflect them to the world.

Have kids rejoin their partners for closing prayer. Partners will pray for each other to reflect the specific Christlike qualities written on their cards.

IN OR OUT?

THEME: Judging Others

All of us are guilty of occasionally jumping to conclusions about people, based on appearances or our own hidden prejudices. Teenagers tend to be even more vulnerable to this tendency. Their search for personal identity often produces a strong need to fit in and to define the limits of who and what are "acceptable."

In this meeting kids will examine some of the effects of prejudice and consider biblical guidelines for relating to those they may be tempted to look down on.

▶ Before the Meeting

Hang a sheet over a door with slits in it for a person to slide their hands through, so no other part of the person will be showing. Prepare a "crazy poster" based on the words of 1 Samuel 16:7. Write each word on a small piece of construction paper and tape the pieces to the wall in a mixed-up jumble.

Gather markers, pencils, paper, several magazines, 3×5 cards and a bowl. Be sure everyone has a copy of *The Youth Bible*.

▶ 1. You're in Good Hands

Separate the guys and girls, with the guys behind the hanging sheet. Use a marker to number the guys' hands, palms up (one number per pair of hands). Have the guys remove any jewelry, then take turns putting their hands through the slits in the hanging sheet, palms up. Give the girls paper and pencils and have them write down who they think owns each pair of hands. Then have the girls write down on their papers the number of the best-looking hands in the group.

Remove the sheet and see if anyone guessed the owners of all the hands correctly. Then collect the girls' papers and announce who got the most votes for "best hands." (Announce only the winner—don't degrade anyone by letting him know he came in last.)

Ask: **Girls, how did it feel to judge the guys' hands on the basis of physical appearance? Boys, how did it feel to be judged? What really makes hands important and valuable? Is physical appearance any indication of the skills hands are capable of performing? Explain. How was judging hands on their appearance like the way some people judge others in real life?**

Say: **Let's think more about what it means to judge others and see what the Bible has to say to us about prejudice.**

▶ 2. Something to Gain?

Ask a volunteer to read aloud the devotion "A Perfect Ten?" (p. 1296 in *The Youth Bible*).

Ask: **What do you think the two boys behind the counter were trying to do? Girls, how would you feel if you were Terri Smith? Guys, how about if YOU were Terri Smith?**

Form three groups and assign each group one of the following devotions and passages from *The Youth Bible*: "Prejudice," John 4:5-42; "The Color of Hatred," Acts 10:34-38; or "Inside Out," Galatians 3:23-29. Ask groups to read through their devotions and passages and discuss the following questions:

● **What do people *gain* when they act out their prejudices toward others?**

● **How does this story and passage teach us to respond to prejudice?**

Allow about 10 minutes for study and discussion. Then bring everyone together and have groups report their findings.

Say: **Prejudiced people often feel good about thinking of themselves as better than others. By putting people down, they try to build themselves up. Let's take a look at another passage that gives us clues about how God feels about prejudice.**

▶ 3. Mixed-Up Message

Distribute paper and pencils. Direct kids' attention to the crazy poster. Challenge them to sort out the verse. When they start to get frustrated, give them the reference, 1 Samuel 16:7.

Give a brief synopsis of the context, then say: **God always looks at what's on the inside. Can you think of any experiences you've had with prejudging someone from appearances only? Explain.**

▶ 4. Picturing Preconceptions

Give a magazine to every three people in the room. Ask the "triplets" to flip through the pages and find pictures of people they might have preconceptions about; for example, physically or mentally disabled people, people of other races, politicians. Have kids each tear out a picture and write on it three preconceptions they would tend to have about the person in the picture.

Form a circle and distribute 3×5 cards. Have kids each write (in private, without writing names) three of their own shortcomings. Then have them fold the cards and place them in a bowl in the middle of the circle.

▶ 5. Scrambled Requests

Gather all of the pictures from the magazines and place them in the bowl too.

Say: **We are now going to have a time of prayer. As you bow your heads, I will call out the prayer requests for you to pray about in silence, based on the things I pull out of this bowl.**

Alternately pull out a picture, then an index card, then a picture, and so on. Give kids a general prayer request based on your selection. For example: **Pray for those who are physically disabled,** or: **Pray for someone here who struggles with lust.**

Assure kids that you will keep the personal shortcomings general so that no one will be identified. Skip or generalize any entries that are too specific.

Close by encouraging kids to look beyond the surface as they meet people this week.

MAKING A DIFFERENCE

THEME: Justice

Most teenagers have an acute sense of justice. Kids may be surprised to find that God cares about justice even more than they do. It can also be an encouragement for them to get to know God better. Use this meeting to help kids gain new insights about God's perspective on justice in what sometimes seems like a very unfair world.

▶ Before the Meeting

Gather a choir robe, a gavel (or rubber mallet), newsprint, markers, tape, paper, pencils, several pairs of scissors and recent newspapers. Make sure you have several copies of *The Youth Bible* on hand.

▶ 1. Mock Justice

Ask for volunteers to be a judge, prosecuting attorney, defense attorney, defendant, jury members and witnesses in a mock trial.

Explain that the defendant is accused of sucking all the jelly out of the jelly doughnuts at the local doughnut shop. If found guilty, the defendant could face 10 years to life washing coffee cups at the shop. Give the judge the robe and gavel. Give the attorneys a minute or so to prepare their cases, and get witnesses for their side.

While the attorneys are preparing their cases, take the jury and judge aside for special instructions. Secretly tell them that no matter what arguments are presented, they are to find the defendant guilty. Then have the judge convene the court. The prosecutor will go first, then the defense; then the judge will ask the jury for a verdict.

After the trial, ask: **In light of the verdict, how do you, the prosecutor, feel? the defense attorney? the defendant?**

Explain that the verdict was rigged from the beginning.

Ask: **How do you feel knowing the trial was rigged?** Get reactions from the class as well as from the principal players in the trial.

Say: **It's upsetting to be treated unjustly. Many people face injustice over issues far heavier than jelly doughnuts. We know that the world is an unjust place. The question is: What can we, as Christians, do to make a difference?**

124

▶ 2. Personal Injustice

Have kids form groups of three.

Say: **We've all heard the expression: Life isn't fair. I want you to share with each other one time life wasn't fair to you— maybe it was an honor you didn't win, a game you lost, or a time you got sick and had to miss a special activity.**

Allow a few minutes for sharing, then pull the group together.

Ask: **How did recalling these experiences make you feel? How did you feel listening to what happened to your friends? Why does a just God allow these things to happen?**

▶ 3. Hall of Justice

Have kids return to their groups. Distribute newsprint and markers. Assign each group one of the following devotions and passages from *The Youth Bible*: "She Died in a Box," Isaiah 9:1-7; "Making a Difference," Amos 8:4-8; or "It's Not Fair," Matthew 20:1-16. After discussing the questions at the end, have groups each write out two or three principles of justice based on their reading.

Encourage the kids to write large, using a whole sheet of newsprint for each principle. Then have them "paper" your room with the principles they have written out, turning it into a "hall of justice."

Say: **It's one thing to understand God's principles of justice; it's another thing to apply them.**

▶ 4. Get on Your Soap Box

Have volunteers read "Quiet Disasters" and Luke 3:1-18 from *The Youth Bible*.

Say: **Your groups of three will now become speech writers bureaus. You have five minutes to write a speech about what John the Baptist would say to a specific audience today. You can choose to have your group's speech aimed at world leaders, our country, our church, our town, your family or your school.**

Hand out paper and pencils. Allow the kids in each group to confer on their choice of audience and write their speech. After five minutes, have a presenter from each group give the prepared speech.

Then ask: **What similarities did you hear in the speeches? How did you feel playing the role of prophet? What responsibilities go with the prophet's role?**

▶ 5. Addressing the Problem

Distribute scissors and a recent newspaper to each student. Have kids search for and clip articles that point out injustice or tell what people are doing to correct injustice. Kids can tape their clipped articles to the hall of justice wall.

Call the group together to look over the articles. Decide which issue to address as a group. Brainstorm strategies for action that could make a difference. List the ideas the kids come up with on newsprint. After several ideas are offered, decide on a course of action.

Close by committing your plans to God in prayer.

WHAT KIND OF LEADER ARE YOU?

THEME: Leadership

Teenagers often associate leadership with authority, bossiness or being an adult and having the freedom to do what you want. The Bible gives us a positive image of leadership that kids need to hear and understand. Biblically, leaders are servants with a unique responsibility to do what is right. Leadership means sacrifice—not asking for "special favors." And all of us, including teenagers, are called to lead in some way. This meeting helps kids understand leadership and decide what kind of leader they will be.

▶ Before the Meeting

Gather three pitchers of water and three glasses, newsprint, markers, pencils and paper. Make sure everyone has a copy of *The Youth Bible*.

▶ 1. Lead Me to Drink

Place three pitchers of water and two glasses on a table in front of the group. Number off three volunteers to participate in a poison water experiment. Assign volunteer 1 as the guardian, volunteer 2 as the taster and volunteer 3 as the ruler.

Say: **One of the pitchers of water before us contains a mild poison. The other two contain ordinary water. In this experiment, the goal is to keep the ruler from being poisoned by the bad water. The guardian will decide which water to test; then the taster will taste the water to see if it's poi-** soned. **If the taster doesn't get sick, the ruler will enjoy a glass of water from that pitcher. If the taster does get sick,** then the guardian must taste water from another pitcher to see if it's safe for the ruler to drink.

Begin the experiment. After the first taste test, check the taster's pulse and look for general signs of poisoning.

After the experiment, ask the three: **How did it feel to be the guardian? the taster? the ruler?** Ask the group: **Which of these three is the leader in this experiment? Explain.**

Say: **Really, all three acted as leaders in different ways. The first made the selection; the second took the risk; and the third commanded the authority and respect of the others. Everyone is a leader in one way or another. Today we'll look at different kinds of leaders and help you decide what kind of leader you want to be.**

2. Leadership Lessons

Form groups of three or more. Assign each group two or three of the following devotions from *The Youth Bible*: "Somebody Do Something," "Walking in My Own Footsteps," "Standing for Right," "Pass the Paintbrush," "Earned Respect," "The Measure of a Leader," "Who'll Pay for It?" "Leading a Just Cause," "Gentle Leadership." (You don't have to use all the devotions.) Have each group choose a scribe. Give each of the scribes a pencil and paper.

Say: **As you read your devotions, look for what really makes a leader. As you discover leadership qualities, your scribes will write them down.**

Allow time for study and discussion, then bring everyone together and have groups share their findings. Record the leadership qualities on newsprint, and praise kids for their insight.

Say: **Now that your group has guidelines for measuring leaders, let's see how some of our better-known Bible leaders hold up under scrutiny.**

3. Bible Profiles

Assign one of these Bible leaders to each group and have them look up the related passages: Moses (Exodus 3:1-20; Deuteronomy 18:15-20), Joshua (Numbers 27:12-23), Deborah (Judges 4:4-16), and David (2 Samuel 5:1-5; 1 Kings 2:1-11). Have groups read their passages and determine how many of the leadership qualities their character demonstrates.

When groups are ready, have them each tell what they came up with.

Then say: **There are many great leaders in the Bible, but even they had their flaws.**

But God made up the difference—and helped them become the leaders he wanted them to be.

Ask: **How did it feel to realize even the Bible leaders weren't perfect? What does that say about your own leadership potential?**

4. Leadership Disaster

Have kids turn to "Fish Out of Water" (p. 1014 in *The Youth Bible*). Read aloud the devotion and Luke 6:39-49, the related scripture passage. Discuss the questions at the end of the devotion.

Ask: **What examples can you give of bad leadership in the human world that has led to the kind of disaster experienced by the whales in this story? How can we overcome bad leadership? In what ways have you been the victim of bad leadership at school? in your personal life?**

5. Lead Me to Drink Again

Remind the kids of the poison experiment you did at the beginning of the meeting.

Say: **According to Jesus, the foundation of all leadership is serving others. He said that whoever wanted to be the greatest must be the servant of all.**

Ask: **Which of the leaders from our experiment was the greatest servant? Based upon what we've learned today, what kinds of leadership qualities do you see in kids in our group?**

Have kids return to their study groups and affirm the leadership qualities they see in one another.

NO GREATER GIFT

THEME: Life

It's a common human tendency to forget that life is a precious gift. We often spend more time complaining about what we don't have than we do thanking God for what we do have. God has given us both physical and eternal life—and that's reason to celebrate!

This meeting encourages kids to consider what it means to live life to the fullest. Seeing all of life as valuable, they can open themselves to more fully experience both the joy and the sadness that will come their way.

Before the Meeting

Gather a large box for each group member, markers, old magazines, newspapers, scissors, glue and crayons. Be sure everyone will have access to a *Youth Bible*.

1. Boxed In?

Place the large boxes in the center of the room. As kids arrive, have them choose a box and take it to a private spot. When everyone has arrived, have kids get *into* their boxes in such a way that they cannot see anyone else. There is to be no talking.

Say: **Suppose you had to live your life in a box. I'm going to give you three minutes to think about what life in a box would be like. You must be silent the whole time. This may seem like an eternity, but do your best.**

At the end of three minutes, toss a marker into each box and ask kids to write down their feelings. They are to write the responses to these questions on three different inside walls of their boxes. Read each question, then give kids time to write their responses.

● **How do you feel about life in a box?**
● **What do you miss?**
● **How is your real life like living in a box?**

When kids are finished writing, have them flip their boxes so the open end is facing the middle of the room. Have kids sit outside the open end of their boxes. The group should now be seated in a large circle, boxes and all. Discuss kids' responses to the questions you asked while they were in the boxes.

Say: **Sometimes we live our lives as if we were in a box. We fail to fully appreciate the gift of life that God has given us. Can you suggest some ways we do this?** Examples might include: not being open to new experiences, only sticking with people who are like ourselves, trying to avoid painful or sad experiences, placing too much value on others' opinions of us.

Say: **We also tend to take for granted the greatest gift that we have received—the life of God's own son, Jesus Christ. Let's look into the Bible as we do a little more thinking about these things.**

▶ **2. Life's a Stage**

Form four groups. Assign each group one of the following devotions and passages from *The Youth Bible*: "The Good Things," Genesis 1:1-31; "A Light in the Darkness," Mark 16:1-8; "Good News," Luke 24:1-11; or "Along for the Ride," John 6:59-69. Have kids read through their devotions and passages and prepare to answer the question: How does your story and passage celebrate life?

Allow time for reading and discussion. Then bring everyone together and have groups share their findings.

Say: **Sometimes it takes a shocking event to make us wake up and appreciate life for what it is. We're pretty lucky if we can get the message without going through any of the trauma!**

▶ **3. The Many Sides of Life**

Dump a large quantity of old magazines and newspapers, scissors and glue into the center of the circle. Have kids turn their boxes open-side-down for stability.

Say: **Find pictures and words that represent the joy we find in living in God's creation. Glue them to one of the outside walls of your box.**

Allow time for kids to find pictures and paste them on their boxes. Then distribute crayons or colored markers.

Say: **On the second side of your box, I want you to draw or write something that represents a time when you experienced a "resurrection" in your life, a time when you were given a second chance or when you gained a new perspective on a problem.**

Give kids a chance to draw or write about their experience.

Say: **On the third side of your box, use a pattern of colors to express the joy and the struggles of your life as a Christian.**

After kids have completed this project, say: **The fourth side of your box is to represent the things you enjoy the most in life. Make it like a mural or a collage. Use pictures from the magazines in addition to your own words and drawings.**

When kids have completed the work on their boxes, have them stroll around the room and enjoy what other people have created. Encourage kids to share and explain the meanings of the images on the walls of their boxes.

Bring the group together and ask: **How would you describe a life that is lived to the fullest? What kind of life would you call a "failure"?**

▶ **4. Lively Litany**

To close, stand in a circle of thanksgiving. Go around the circle, having kids call out something in their lives for which they are thankful. After each statement, the group will enthusiastically respond "Oh, yeah!"

NEVER ALONE

THEME: Loneliness

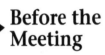

Before the Meeting

Gather large, paper grocery bags, paper, pencils and a copy of *The Youth Bible* for each student. Write a relational task for each student on a 3×5 card. Choose from the ideas below or make up your own. If your group is larger than twelve, you may want to use the same idea for more than one student.

- Find out from three people what they like on their pizza.
- Let someone know what makes you really sad.
- Share the funniest joke you've heard recently.
- Guess the shoe size of two people; get a high five if you're right.
- Get someone to rub your shoulders.
- Ask two people about the last good movie they saw.
- Let someone know that you want your back scratched.
- Ask two people about their favorite vacation

Loneliness can hit in the most diverse places—a barren desert, a hospital waiting room or a roomful of apparently happy, busy people. Kids in today's mobile society are especially vulnerable to painful feelings of isolation. This meeting will help kids see that God is concerned about their loneliness and that the scriptures offer hope through deeper relationships with God and his people.

ever; tell about yours.
- Discover the most unfavorite foods of three people.
- Tell someone how you would feel about taking skydiving lessons.
- Demonstrate to someone how you act when you're embarrassed.
- Tell someone what happened the last time you were really scared.

1. In the Bag

As kids arrive, give them each a 3×5 card with one of the above tasks written on it. Have them keep their cards hidden and their tasks a secret. Distribute paper bags.

Say: **The particular challenge of this activity is to accomplish your task while you're wearing a paper bag over your head. Ready? It's bag time!**

Give kids a few minutes to mingle and accomplish their tasks.

Then say: **Okay—it's time to de-bag.**

130

Ask: **How did it feel trying to accomplish your task with a bag over your head? What difference did the bag make in the way you related to people? In what ways did this exercise demonstrate what loneliness is like? What did this activity show you about the importance of reaching out to people?**

▶ 2. So Alone

Form three groups. Assign one of the following devotions and passages from *The Youth Bible* to each group: "You Against the World," 1 Kings 19:11-18; "On the Road Again," Psalm 68:1-10; or "Left, But Not Forgotten," Psalm 137:1-6.

Have kids within each group read the devotion and passage aloud. Then have them discuss the cause of loneliness for the character in their devotion and tell what consolation or hope the Bible offers.

Bring everyone together and have groups each report on their story and on the hope offered in their passage.

Ask: **Were the people in these stories responsible for their own loneliness? Explain. When have you experienced this kind of loneliness? Which of these passages of** hope from the Bible is the most meaningful to you?

▶ 3. The Good Side

Have kids return to their three groups and read the passages listed under the "For More, See …" section of their devotion.

Say: **As you read through these passages, look for the good things that can come out of lonely times. Brainstorm a list of the positive results of loneliness.**

After a few minutes, call the groups together and have them share the results of their search.

▶ 4. Solutions

Gather kids in a circle and distribute 3×5 cards and pencils. Have kids each write down one idea for overcoming loneliness, then toss their card into a pile in the center of the circle. Shuffle the cards and have kids each pick one.

Say: **Read the suggestion on your card aloud, then tell if you think it's realistic and if you might consider trying it during a lonely time in the future.**

Close with prayer, asking God for courage to reach out when we sense a need for companionship in ourselves or in others.

MORE THAN FLOWERS AND CANDY

THEME: Love

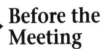

> **Y**our teenagers may be surprised to learn that biblical love has more to do with choices than feelings. But as the realization dawns on them that God loves them no matter what they do, they will be more inclined to give their love freely to others. Use this meeting to help your kids understand the practical aspects of passing on God's love.

Before the Meeting

Gather a piece of strong garlic bread, a roll of breath mints, newsprint, markers, tape, pencils and 3×5 cards. Make sure everyone has a copy of *The Youth Bible*.

1. Take a Breather!

Ask for a volunteer who's willing to do something that's just the slightest bit gross. (Make sure your volunteer is a confident, outgoing person.) In front of all the other kids, have the volunteer eat a piece of garlic bread that you've loaded with extra garlic.

Say to the volunteer: **I really appreciate your willingness to help out. It was probably pretty gross eating that strong garlic bread. Now, since you're such a friendly person, I want you to go around to everyone and say, "Here's a hug and a hearty hello."** Be sure to emphasize all the h's so

people will get a whiff of the true flavor of your friendship.

Say to the rest of the group: **I want you to show your appreciation for (name)'s cooperation by giving (him or her) a hearty hug in return.**

There will probably be a great deal of amusement as the volunteer's garlic-breath affection is spread around the group. When everyone has received a greeting and a hug, reward the volunteer with a round of applause and a roll of breath mints.

Ask: **How did you feel about getting a garlic greeting? How is this like not wanting to get close to certain people in real life? What are the big turn-offs for you when it comes to meeting people?**

This last question could raise some hurtful issues for kids, but it also offers some important opportunities for growth. Be careful not to let it turn into a put-down session. Some members might mention acne or obesity as being turn-offs—and you might have kids in your group who have acne or a weight problem. Deal with this issue gently, by asking if it's fair or right to judge people for things they have little or no control over.

Then ask: **Do you think most people tend to give love on the basis of how lovable other people are? Explain. How does that line up with your understanding of Christian love?**

Have kids turn to 1 John 4:7-12 in *The Youth Bible*. Ask volunteers to read the passage and the related devotion "The First Step" aloud.

Say: **In the devotion, Angie says: "Loving people who love us is easy. Loving difficult people makes Christian love unique." Do you agree or disagree with that statement? Explain.**

Tell kids this meeting is about the meaning of love—particularly the love Christians are to have for others.

2. Love Do's and Don'ts

Direct kids' attention to the devotion "Love Never Ends" (p. 1185 in *The Youth Bible*). Have someone read it aloud. Then form two groups and give each group newsprint and a marker. Have both groups read 1 Corinthians 13:4-7. Have one group list the things love does do and the other group list the things love doesn't do. When the groups have finished, have them tape their lists to the wall.

Ask: **In which of these ways did Lisa demonstrate love?**

Put an "L" next to the things on the list as kids name and explain them.

Ask: **In what ways did Gregg demonstrate what love isn't?**

Put a "G" next to the actions on the other list that kids mention.

Ask: **What kind of love did Gregg's father have? Explain.**

Read aloud the story of Rochelle from the devotion "Given, Not Earned" (p. 1304 in *The Youth Bible*).

Then ask: **Do you think dads typically act the way the father in this story acted? Give an example from your own experience to support your answer.**

Have a volunteer read aloud 1 Peter 1:17-23. Then ask the first question at the end of the devotion, regarding how Rochelle's dad's love for her is like God's love for us. You may wish to take this opportunity to give a brief explanation of the gospel message, focusing on 1 Peter 1:18-19.

▶ 3. Check Your Love Level

Say: **We've seen how the Bible speaks about God's unconditional love for us. But did you know that the Bible also talks about the romantic side of love?**

Have kids turn to Song of Solomon 2:10-17 in *The Youth Bible* and read the passage silently. Then direct their attention to the related devotion "Am I Really in Love?" Read the devotion out loud to the kids, pausing after each sentence. Discuss the questions at the end of the devotion. Then lead kids in the second "Consider . . ." activity.

▶ 4. Clearing Away Distractions

Say: **It's interesting to see how two people in love are so focused on each other. The Bible challenges us to keep that kind of passionate focus in our relationship to God.**

Have a volunteer read aloud the devotion "Keeping in Focus" (p. 1176 in *The Youth Bible*). Hand out 3×5 cards and pencils. Explain that you're going to have three minutes of silent prayer in which kids are to ask God to reveal any distractions in their lives that keep them from focusing their love on him. Have kids write any thoughts that come to them on their cards.

Close with a brief prayer of celebration and thankfulness for God's unconditional love and for a willingness to pass that love on to others.

THE MATING GAME

THEME: Marriage

To some people in our society, marriage has become a dirty word. It conjures up feelings of entrapment, burdensome restrictions and closed-mindedness. And that can be what happens when marriage is distorted from God's ideal. Kids need to see that God has a very positive ideal for marriage, an ideal that includes intimacy, fun and the ability to overcome problems together. This meeting encourages kids to see marriage through God's eyes and shows them how they can prepare for this awesome gift from God.

Before the Meeting

Label a large bucket "Society" and fill it with water and a half-cup of bleach. Make photocopies of the "Perfect Mate" handout for each person. Also create a paper-chain link for each person by cutting 9-by-12-inch construction paper into 3-by-12-inch strips. Gather a plastic tablecloth, old white cloth handkerchiefs (or squares of white cloth), permanent markers, washable markers, newsprint, tape, glue-sticks, paper and pencils. Make sure everyone has a copy of *The Youth Bible*.

1. Fading Convictions

Give kids each a handkerchief and a permanent marker. On their cloths, have kids each write two words that describe marriage. When kids are finished, collect the permanent markers and distribute washable markers. Have kids each write two more words that describe marriage. When everyone is finished, have volunteers tell what they wrote and why. Then spread the plastic tablecloth on the floor and put on it the bucket labeled "Society." Have kids drop their handkerchiefs in the bucket. Swish the handkerchiefs around for a couple of minutes, then take them out one by one, wringing them out to keep from dripping on the floor. The comments written in washable marker will be faded or gone.

Return the handkerchiefs to their owners and ask: **How did you feel about the words you wrote? Explain. How did you feel when you saw some of the words washing away? How is this experience like marriage in today's society?**

Say: **Society can steal away the values that help hold marriages together. In fact, society has gained such a negative view of marriage that many people now question whether anyone should ever get married.**

▶ 2. To Marry or Not to Marry

Form two groups. Read aloud the "One Body … Kind Of" devotion (p. 5 in *The Youth Bible*). Then lead a debate about whether Jeff and Connie should get married. Designate one group as the Should Marry and the other group as the Should Not Marry. Have groups each come up with as many reasons as possible that support their position. When groups are ready, have them take turns reading aloud one reason at a time, discussing its validity as they go. Continue until one group runs out of reasons.

Ask: **How did it feel debating your side of the issue? Do you think marriages were meant to last until death? Why or why not?**

Say: **According to the Bible, when a marriage is based on biblical principles, it will hold together for life. To study this further, let's talk about two essentials to any marriage—faith and commitment.**

▶ 3. Success Stories

Keep kids in the same groups and assign each group one of the following devotions from *The Youth Bible*: "Ask Her, John" (p. 242) or "Like Great-Grandmother" (p. 595). Have groups each read their devotion, then provide paper and pencils so groups can list the qualities that made that marriage successful. When groups are finished, bring everyone together and compare the lists.

Then have volunteers read aloud these Bible passages: Genesis 2:18-24; Genesis 29:16-20; Ruth 4:7-17; and Matthew 19:3-6. Using the principles from the stories and passages, work as a whole group to come up with a Christian definition of marriage.

Say: **When we walk with God, marriage becomes an exciting possibility for us to look forward to. And it just might come more quickly than you think.**

▶ 4. The Perfect Mate

Say: **Marriage may seem like a long way off, but the preparation and decision-making begin now. Are your dates potential mates? Let's find out.**

Give kids each a photocopy of the handout "The Perfect Mate" and have them work individually to rank the qualities they would like in their future spouse. When everyone is finished, have volunteers tell their top two and bottom two choices and explain why they chose as they did.

Choose kids to read aloud Proverbs 31:10-31; Ephesians 5:21-33; and 1 Peter 3:1-7.

After each scripture is read, have kids brainstorm qualities of a godly husband or wife. Write their responses on newsprint.

Say: **Now that we know a little bit about what our mates should be like, let's close by considering what kind of mate we would be for someone else.**

▶ 5. Personal Possibilities

Give each person a paper chain link and a marker. On one side, have kids write a quality they already have that makes them a good potential mate. On the other side, have them write a quality they need to build into their lives to be a better potential mate.

When everyone is finished, have kids form a circle. Pass around gluesticks so kids can make a paper chain from their links. As they make the chain, tell kids to pray silently that the person on their right would have God's help making wise choices about dating, marriage or remaining single.

Once the chain is complete, hang it on the wall as a reminder of God's goodness in linking our hearts in close relationships with each other.

Close with prayer.

THE Perfect Mate

Rank the qualities you would like to see in a potential mate from one to 11, with one being the highest and 11 being the lowest.

_____ has a sense of humor

_____ is great looking

_____ has good parenting skills

_____ has a strong commitment to Christ

_____ is dependable and honest

_____ has similar interests

_____ is a good lover

_____ is intelligent

_____ has a good job

_____ is an effective communicator

_____ is committed to making the marriage work

BIG BUCKS—THE BIG PICTURE

THEME: Money

Kids need to see it's not the Donald Trumps of this world who deserve our admiration as financial heroes. The real heroes are those who use their money to accomplish God's purposes. This meeting will help kids give careful thought to how to control their money, rather than letting money control them.

Before the Meeting

Gather a balloon, pencils and photocopies of the "Money: Get a Grip On It" handout. Make sure you have a copy of *The Youth Bible* for each group member.

1. Happiness Toss

Gather kids in a circle. Blow up a balloon. Explain that you're going to toss the balloon. The person who catches it will finish the sentence: I would be really happy if ... That person will then toss it to another person, and so on until everyone has finished the sentence.

Have kids sit down, then ask: **What patterns did you see emerging in the responses people gave? How many of the things we mentioned had to do with money? How much do you think money is involved with our personal happiness?**

Read aloud the devotion "What's Important?"

(p. 984 in *The Youth Bible*).

Then ask: **Why can't money deliver what it promises? What happens when we depend on money for happiness? for security? How does money affect your faith? your actions?**

Read aloud Zephaniah 1:7-18 and Mark 10:17-30.

Ask: **What do these passages say about the limitations of money? about the bondage of money?**

2. Models to Bank On

Form three groups. Assign each group one of the following devotions and passages from *The Youth Bible*: "It's Only Money," Luke 12:32-40; "Tool or Master?" Luke 16:1-13; or "Earning Potential," Luke 19:11-27. Have groups each search for three principles about money in their story and passage.

Allow about 10 minutes for study and discussion. Then bring everyone together. Have groups each summarize their story and tell the three principles about money they discovered.

Ask: **What challenges did these people face in using their money the way God wanted them to? What helped them carry through on their resolve?**

Say: **Of course, God doesn't want us to try to make ourselves famous by our sacrificial giving. But he does want us to look carefully at the choices we make and the goals we set regarding money. Will we seek to use money for money's sake or to minister with it? Will we hoard it or use it to accomplish God's purposes?**

▶ 3. The Purpose of Money

Read aloud the devotion "More and More" (p. 1260 in *The Youth Bible*). Ask: **When have you felt like Janice? Explain. How can you guard against money—or the longing for things money can buy—taking control of your life?**

Ask a volunteer to read aloud the related passage, 1 Timothy 6:1-16. Then discuss the questions at the end of the devotion.

4. Get a Grip on It

Distribute pencils and photocopies of the handout "Money: Get a Grip on It." Have a volunteer read aloud Hebrews 13:5-6. Then allow time for kids to complete the handout individually.

Ask: **Did you make any surprising discoveries in your personal financial inventory? Explain. What positive financial changes did you plan?**

▶ 5. Toss It Again

Form a circle for another game of balloon toss. Explain that this time, kids who catch the balloon will tell one non-material thing that makes them happy.

Close with prayer, acknowledging God as the source of all things and asking his help in using money responsibly.

MONEY: GET A GRIP ON IT!

Read Hebrews 13:5-6. Then complete the personal financial review below.

My average monthly income:

My average monthly spending:

My average monthly savings:

My average monthly giving:

One thing I've learned today from the Bible about money is . . .

One thing I feel really good about in my use of money is . . .

One thing I need to change in my use of money is . . .

HIDE OR SEEK?

THEME: Non-Christians

Many kids who've been raised in a strongly Christian environment don't have the faintest idea where to begin building friendships with non-Christians. Some are even taught to avoid non-Christians entirely. In this meeting, kids will explore what scripture says about associating with people outside our own faith and discover starting points from which they may genuinely share their faith with those who need to hear about God.

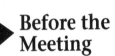

Before the Meeting

Make sure you have a copy of *The Youth Bible* for each group member.

1. Trivia Tumble

Arrange chairs in a circle, with one fewer chairs than there are people. Have the person who is wearing the most red be "It" and stand in the middle of the circle. Explain that this game works something like Fruit Basket Upset. "It" will call out a well-known person, place or thing. The rest of the group must immediately shout out a related word—something they think other kids will say too. For example, if "It" were to call out "baseball," other kids might yell "bat," "pitcher" or "home run."

Kids have to keep shouting their word loudly while "It" counts to ten. The group members must listen for someone else in the circle who is shouting the same thing they are and quickly change seats with that person when the count reaches 10. "It" will try to grab an empty seat during the switch. The person left in the middle becomes the new "It."

After playing a few rounds, ask: **How did it feel to stand in the middle? How did it feel when you heard someone else saying the same thing you said?**

Say: **The most effective way to make friends is to listen to what other people are saying and match our interests to theirs. That's one way to build a bridge of friendship so that we can eventually share our faith in Christ.**

2. Plain Speaking

Have kids turn to Acts 17:22-31 in *The Youth Bible*.

Before a volunteer reads the passage aloud, say: **Imagine you are hearing about God for the first time. How much of this speech** would you understand?

After the passage has been read, ask: **Did you hear a lot of fancy theological language in this speech? What tactics did Paul use to build bridges to these people? What could you learn from Paul's approach? Have you ever been confused or put off by someone who used a lot of religious terms you didn't understand? Explain. How can we avoid making the same mistake when we're talking to non-Christian friends?**

 ## 3. Familiar God Phrases

Form two groups. Have group 1 look up 2 Corinthians 6:14-18. Have group 2 look up Matthew 9:9-13. Have groups each appoint a team leader and prepare a debate based on their passage. Group 1 will be in favor of avoiding non-believers; group 2 will support spending time with non-believers. Allow five minutes for groups to prepare their arguments.

Serve as timekeeper, allowing each group three minutes to present its case.

Then say: **Paul advises Christians to avoid too much contact with non-Christians. Yet Jesus spent a great deal of time with non-believers. How can we resolve this apparent conflict?**

Ask a volunteer to read aloud the devotion "Beyond the Great Divide" (p. 1016 in *The Youth Bible*).

Ask: **If Jesus were a student at your school, who might he spend the most time with?** Then read aloud the devotion "Trying Too Hard" (p. 1195 in *The Youth Bible*) and encourage kids to suggest ways Dave could share his faith in a less irritating manner.

4. Unique Approaches

Have kids turn to the devotion "A Starting Place" (p. 1126 in *The Youth Bible*). Ask three kids to read aloud the first three paragraphs.

Then lead the group in the second "Consider ..." activity. Have kids pair off. Then have partners tell each other about one friend they'd like to introduce to Jesus. Have partners brainstorm ways to share the truth about Jesus with those people in meaningful ways.

Have partners pray for each other that they will be able to share Christ effectively with the specific friend they mentioned.

5. Into the World

Have group members form a circle facing outward and join hands. Stand in the middle of the circle and read Jesus' great commission from Mark 16:15-16. Then dismiss kids with the words "Go in God's grace and power."

HANG ON

THEME: Patience

Patience levels fluctuate pretty drastically in the lives of most teenagers. Some days they seem calm, controlled and mature. Other days there's a burst of temper if things don't happen right now. It's tough for kids to hold on to the reins of youthful energy and enthusiasm. In this meeting, kids will discover the biblical meaning of patience and learn the value of waiting for God's perfect timing.

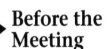

Before the Meeting

Gather four inflated balloons of different colors, newsprint, markers, pencils and masking tape. Make sure everyone has a copy of *The Youth Bible*.

1. Balloon Bedlam

Arrange the chairs in a tight circle. Have kids sit close together and extend their feet and legs into the center of the circle with heels resting on the floor and toes pointed up. Place a balloon on someone's outstretched ankles. Explain that you're going to yell "right" or "left." The person holding the balloon will lift the balloon over the legs of the next person in that direction, then drop the balloon by opening his or her feet. Kids will continue passing the balloon around the circle in this manner until it comes back to the person who started it.

Meanwhile, give another balloon to someone on the other side of the circle. Start this one in the opposite direction. When the two balloons meet, the kids who are holding them will have to pass the balloons very carefully in opposite directions.

Just when kids are getting used to this, give another balloon to still another person, but this time have kids use their hands to pass the balloon. Start a fourth balloon in the opposite direction of the third one; kids will also use their hands to pass this one. Kids will need to keep track of the different balloons by color. You can make the game more exciting by explaining that letting a balloon touch the floor means "instant death" (leaving the circle).

After a few minutes, ask: **How did you feel when several balloons were headed in your direction? How did you feel when you had to pass two or more balloons in different directions at the same time? What would you say was the key to passing the balloons?** (To pass them slowly and carefully.) **How does it make you feel when you have** to be slow and careful and patient about things? What kinds of things require patience in real life? How would you rate your own patience level?

Say: **In this meeting we are going to consider how patient (or impatient) we are and look at some of the rewards that come with being patient.**

2. Patience Pays

Form four groups (a group may be as small as one person). Assign each group one of the following devotions and passages from *The Youth Bible*: "He's Still at Work," Isaiah 62:1-12; "Pumping Iron," Habakkuk 2:1-4; "Looking Back," Romans 8:22-30; or "Endless Paddling," James 5:7-11. Tell kids their task is to develop answers to these two questions to share later with the whole group: What's so tough about being patient? What's rewarding about being patient? Have kids give a specific example from their devotion and passage.

Allow a few minutes for study and discussion. Then bring everyone together and have groups report their findings.

Ask: **What advice would you give someone who struggles with impatience? Explain.**

3. Facing Frustration

Have volunteers read the devotion "When the Going Gets Tough," (p. 75 in *The Youth Bible*) and the related scripture passage, Exodus 17:1-7. Discuss the questions at the end of the devotion.

Ask: **Have you ever felt as desperately impatient as the Israelites? Explain. Have you ever been with a group of people who functioned as well in a frustrating situation as the kids in the story did? What's the key to patience in a situation like that?**

4. Cloudy Futures

Distribute newsprint and markers. Have kids each tear a cloud from the newsprint.

Say: **This cloud represents something on** the horizon of your life, some goal or event you're waiting for. Write your name in large letters at the top of your cloud. Then write on your cloud several specific things you're patiently waiting for.

Have kids turn to "Worth the Wait" (p. 1265 in *The Youth Bible*). Ask volunteers to read aloud the devotion and the related scripture passage, 2 Timothy 2:8-13.

Ask: **What was the key to Rosa's success? What would have happened if Rosa had not been so persistent? How are the patience and suffering mentioned in this scripture passage like the patience and suffering of blacks during the boycott? How could this passage help you be more patient waiting for the things you really want to happen?**

Have kids put a star by the "waiting item" on their cloud that is the hardest for them to wait for right now. Then have kids stand on chairs and hang their clouds on the wall.

5. Words of Encouragement

While kids are still standing on their chairs, ask them to "dream" about where they would like to be or what they would like to be doing in the next five to 10 years. Encourage everyone to be specific.

Say: **One of the things that's most effective in combating impatience is getting encouragement from Christian friends.**

Explain that on your signal, kids are to climb on other kids' chairs and write a short note of encouragement on each person's cloud. Say "go!" and allow a few minutes for kids to write on each other's clouds. When everyone has finished, have kids take down their own clouds.

Say: **Look back through the scripture passages we've studied today and choose a verse that will encourage you to be patient and trust in God's timing. Write that verse on your cloud.**

Have kids take their clouds home and hang them where they can be a daily source of encouragement.

Close with the song "In His Time."

143

BEYOND UNDERSTANDING

THEME: Peace

Imagine ... You always agree with your friends ... You never argue with your parents ... At school students are eager to learn and teachers are fair ... There are no losers in sports ... The news reports another day of trust and cooperation among people throughout the world.

Our world is not like that. Conflict surrounds us. It is part of our lives. God's Word teaches us something different. In Jesus we have a peace that passes *all* understanding. Kids need to see that they can have God's peace in their lives despite negative circumstances.

▶ Before the Meeting

Gather about four dozen balloons, tape, newsprint, markers and two or three dictionaries. Make sure you have copies of *The Youth Bible* for each student.

▶ 1. Peace or Pieces?

Have kids form five pairs or small groups (a group can be one person). Give each group several balloons and a roll of tape. Explain that they are to blow up and connect the balloons to form a letter. Whisper one letter of the word "Peace" to each group but keep the word a secret.

When groups each complete their letter, have them bring it to the center of the room. Have kids guess what word the letters form, then arrange the letters in the right order on the floor.

Say: **Good work! I know you invested a lot of hot air in these letters. Now I'm going to** let you expend a little more energy. **When I say "go," I want to see which group can be the quickest to destroy another group's** letter. Ready? Go!

After the popping and panting, ask: **How did you feel wrecking someone's letter? How did it feel to see your own letter destroyed? How is this like the way peace is destroyed in our world? in our lives? Why is peace so fragile? Would you be interested in trying to reconstruct the "peace" you just destroyed? Explain. How would that be like trying to regain a sense of peace in your life after something devastating happens to you?**

▶ 2. By Definition

Have kids form three groups. Distribute large sheets of newsprint and markers. Assign each group one of the following passages: Numbers

6:22-27; John 14:15-29; and Philippians 4:1-9.

Say: **Based on your passage, come up with a group definition of peace. Write your definition on the sheet of newsprint and tape it to the wall.**

Bring the groups together. Have kids compare their definitions. Then read aloud definitions of peace from two or three dictionaries. Work together as a whole group to compile a definition everyone agrees on.

Say: **It can be hard enough just to define peace, not to mention hanging onto it in our lives. Let's see how some real people achieved a sense of peace despite difficult circumstances.**

▶ 3. In Spite of It All

Have groups read the devotions that accompany the passages they read in activity 2, and answer the questions at the end.

Bring the groups together and have them share their stories.

Ask: **What did these characters have in common that helped them achieve peace in their lives? Can you visualize yourself with that kind of peace in those circumstances? Explain.**

▶ 4. Peaceful Alternatives

Say: **We often think it's outside circumstances that disturb the peace in our lives. At some point we need to assume responsibility for our reaction to those circumstances and realize that we can either keep the peace—or not.**

Have kids return to their groups. Assign each group one of the following devotions from *The Youth Bible*: "Sibling Rivalry" (p. 619), "The Second Mile" (p. 917), and "Enemy in My House" (p. 1219). Have groups look for what disturbed the peace in the lives of their characters.

Bring groups together and have them share their stories.

Then ask: **What usually disturbs the peace in your life? What really upsets you? Under what circumstances do you find yourself worrying, or constantly in conflict with others?**

Record kids' responses on a sheet of newsprint. Then have a volunteer from each group read aloud the passage that accompanied their devotion: Isaiah 2:1-5; Matthew 5:38-48; and Ephesians 2:4-22.

Based on the passages, have groups brainstorm peaceful alternatives to the responses of conflict or worry.

▶ 5. The Gift of Peace

Say: **I want to close the meeting today by having us share an ancient Christian blessing with one another. Shake hands with each person in the group. One of you will say, "The peace of Christ be with you." The other person will respond, "And with your spirit."**

After kids have "passed the peace," have them stand in a circle as you read Numbers 6:22-27 as a benediction.

145

BEAT THE SQUEEZE

THEME: Peer Pressure

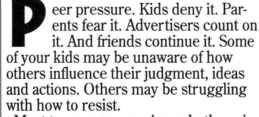

Peer pressure. Kids deny it. Parents fear it. Advertisers count on it. And friends continue it. Some of your kids may be unaware of how others influence their judgment, ideas and actions. Others may be struggling with how to resist.

Most teenagers experience both positive and negative peer pressure. As kids examine the power of peer pressure, help them discover ways to avoid the negative and emphasize the positive.

▶ Before the Meeting

Write the numbers from one to 10 on separate sheets of paper. Gather tape, newsprint, markers, pencils and paper and extra copies of *The Youth Bible*.

▶ 1. Pressure in Action

Tape the 10 numbered sheets in order across the floor, leaving space between each number. Point out the continuum to the kids.

Say: **Number one represents no pressure; number ten represents lots of pressure. The other numbers indicate degrees of pressure. I'll read some questions. After each one, stand beside the number that indicates how much pressure you feel.**

1. **How pressured do you feel to cheat at school?**
2. **How pressured do you feel to cut classes?**
3. **How pressured do you feel to drink?**
4. **How pressured do you feel to have sex?**
5. **How pressured do you feel to own the hottest new album, the latest clothing, or the newest fad?**
6. **How pressured did you feel to go along with where the others stood on this continuum?**

After you read each question, give kids a chance to take a place on the continuum. Then ask each person why they chose to stand in that particular spot.

Say: **Everyone is pressured by friends in some way. Let's look at how pressure affected some people in the Bible.**

▶ 2. An Age-Old Problem

Form four groups (a group can be one person). Assign each group one of the following passages from *The Youth Bible*: Psalm 1; Jeremiah 26:8-15; Mark 15:1-20; or Luke 21:5-

19. Give each group a large sheet of newsprint and a marker.

Say: **Write "Pressure" down the center of the newsprint. Make an acrostic that tells about how pressure is handled in your Bible passage. You can use the letters in the word "pressure" anywhere in the words of your acrostic. Also select a key verse that sums up your passage.**

Here is a sample acrostic from Psalm 1:

```
       HA P PY
    LIKE T R EES
LOVES GOD'S T E ACHINGS
    THINK S ABOUT THEM
         S TRONG
       S U CCEEDS
       F R UITFUL
  PROT E CTED BY GOD
```

After a few minutes, call on each group to share its acrostic and key verse.

Ask: **How do kids today put pressure on each other at school? At church? What are some examples of negative peer pressure? What is positive peer pressure?**

▶ 3. Peer Pressure Update

Use the same four groups. Assign each group the devotion in *The Youth Bible* related to the passage they just read. Have kids prepare a brief skit based on the story in the devotion.

After each group's skit, ask the audience: **What kind of peer pressure was used?**

Ask the group who worked on the skit: **How does this peer pressure skit relate to the verses you studied?**

When all the groups have performed, ask: **What ideas about handling peer pressure did you learn from the skits?**

▶ 4. Emphasize the Positive

Have kids turn to the "Consider ... " ideas following "The K.C. Kid" (p. 482) and "Quick Comeback" (p. 721). Point out the second idea in each section.

Say: **Select one idea from these two. Get together in groups of two or three to complete the activity.**

Provide pencils and paper. After a few minutes ask for volunteers to share their songs or contracts.

Ask: **How can you exert positive peer pressure on others? How do you know if peer pressure is positive or negative?**

▶ 5. Pressure Points

Form two equal-size groups. Ask half the kids to make a circle, then turn outward. Instruct the others to form a circle around the first group and to face inward. Everyone in the outside circle should be standing in front of someone in the inner circle.

Say: **I'll read an incomplete sentence. The person in the center circle has ten seconds to complete the sentence. I'll call time. Then the person in the outside circle has ten seconds to complete the sentence. After the second "time," everyone in the outer circle will shift one person to the right.**

- **The way I feel about peer pressure is ...**
- **I do feel some pressure to ...**
- **I don't feel any pressure to ...**
- **I think I can be a positive friend because I ...**
- **The best advice I could give someone who feels pressured by others is ...**

Close by asking kids to form one large circle and link arms to symbolize the strength that comes from positive peer pressure. Ask them to say sentence prayers asking for strength to face certain kinds of pressure.

HANG IN THERE

THEME: Persistence

Pop Tarts for breakfast. A Big Mac at lunch. And a frozen dinner in the microwave. Teenagers are used to quick gratification of many of their desires. And our "instant culture" teaches them that's the way it should be. But many good things come only with time, effort and persistence. Help your kids see that persistence is often the key to things that bring true joy in life.

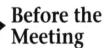

Before the Meeting

For activity 1, hide a few things around the room that will help kids with difficult letters. For example, you might hide a child's xylophone, a picture of a zebra and a quart jar. You may also want to bring prizes for the first two finishers. Gather paper, pencils, 3×5 cards, magazines, scissors and glue. Make sure everyone has a copy of *The Youth Bible*.

1. ABCs of Persistence

Give kids each a sheet of paper and a pencil. Have them each write the alphabet down the left side of their paper. If they don't have room, they can start another column down the middle of the paper.

Then say: **Here's a challenge for you. On "go," find things in this room that begin with each letter of the alphabet and write those items on your sheet next to the ap-**propriate letter. **Feel free to be creative. For example, if we had a huge eraser in this room, you could put "giant eraser" for "g." If you find something unusual, don't tell anyone else because the person with the most completed letters wins.**

Say "go," and let kids search until four or five kids say they've completed the list. If the search goes on for more than six or seven minutes, call time.

Go over the lists of the first two people who finished or had the most completed letters.

Then ask: **How did you find all the things you did? Did any of you just give up? Did you accomplish anything by giving up? Explain.**

Give prizes to the winners if you wish.

Then say: **Those of you who did well did so by keeping at it, working hard, not giving up—by being persistent. Today we're going to see what persistence does for us.**

▶ 2. Group Persistence

Form three groups. Assign each group two of the following devotions and passages from *The Youth Bible*: "What Do You See?" Daniel 7:9-14; "Go for the Gold," Matthew 15:21-28; "The Long Run," Mark 10:46-52; "Sticking With It," Philippians 3:12-21; "Dream Big," 2 Timothy 4:6-8; and "Learning to Win," Hebrews 12:1-13.

Say: **From your passages, devotions and questions, come up with a list of things that explain what it means to be persistent. Make your list as long as you can.**

When groups are done, have them each report by summarizing their passages and devotions and reading their list.

Say: **You did a good job coming up with what persistence is. Some of you probably took this activity more seriously than others. Some of you were more persistent than others.**

▶ 3. Persistent Life

If you have more than 12 kids, form groups of 12 or fewer for the following discussion.

Ask: **Who got the most out of the activity? Why? In life, who gets the most out of Bible study? out of sports? out of serving God? out of going to school? How can we have the kind of persistence we've seen illustrated and talked about in the Bible?**

Let kids discuss the last question for a while. Encourage them to give specifics. Seek participation from all class members. If you formed groups, let groups each report what they discussed.

▶ 4. Practicing Persistence

Give kids 3×5 cards, scissors and old magazines. Have kids each search through a magazine, cut out the letters to spell persistence and glue them to their 3×5 card in order. No two letters can come from the same page.

When kids have finished that, have them look at the "Consider ... " sections of the following devotions from *The Youth Bible* to see what actions are suggested for encouraging persistence: "What Do You See?" (p. 815); "Sticking With It" (p. 1234); "Dream Big" (p. 1267); and "Learning to Win" (p. 1289).

Then have kids each write on the back of their persistence card one way they're going to encourage persistence in their own life or in someone else's. Have kids each take their card home to remind them of the importance of persistence.

Close with prayer, thanking God for his persistence in caring for us.

IN, OUT OR IN BETWEEN?

THEME: Popularity

Kids are quick to learn that getting ahead in life often depends on who you know or, rather, who knows you. But the popularity game never really delivers what it promises. Being a "hot name" on campus can't take the place of being loved and accepted for who you are. This meeting points out the pitfalls in striving for popularity with people, and helps kids see that being recognized by God rather than by people is what counts in the end.

▶ Before the Meeting

Gather newsprint, tape, markers, pencils, paper and posterboard. If you can, get a tape player and the cassette album *Real Life Conversations* by Steven Curtis Chapman. Cue up the song "The Human Race." Make sure everyone has a copy of *The Youth Bible*.

▶ 1. Who's Cliquing?

As kids arrive, tape a sheet of newsprint to the wall and title it "Popular Demands." Have kids brainstorm groups of people at school who tend to stick together, such as athletes, cheerleaders, drama people and cowboys. Write kids' ideas in a line across the top of the newsprint, creating columns under each grouping.

Then ask: **In each of these groups, what does it take to be popular? List kids' responses under the appropriate headings.**

Then say: **Today we're going to look at popularity and see what the Bible has to say about it.**

▶ 2. Shut Out

Have kids form a tight circle. Choose two people to be excluded from the circle. The two "Outs" will try any means possible to get inside the circle. The kids in the circle will try to keep them out. If any of the "Outs" break in, the people who let them in become the new "Outs."

Play two or three rounds of the game. If the "Outs" aren't able to break into the circle, cut off the game after just a couple of minutes.

Ask: **How did it feel trying to break into the circle? How is that like trying to break into a clique of popular kids? How did it feel trying to keep people out of the circle? How is that like belonging to a clique? What's good about belonging to a clique?**

What's bad about it? What's the worst thing about being an outsider?

Say: **Popularity gives us a sense of belonging and helps us believe we are valued by others. But the price of popularity can be high—maybe too high. Let's take a few minutes to discover what we can about God's perspective on popularity.**

▶ 3. Divine Appraisals

Have a volunteer read aloud Mark 9:30-37. Ask kids to brainstorm qualities that would make people "popular" with God. List the responses on newsprint. Then have another volunteer read aloud the related devotion, "Everyone Is Going" (p. 981 in *The Youth Bible*).

Ask: **How popular is Sam from God's perspective? Explain. How popular might Sam become in school as a result of his actions? Explain. What would you have done in Sam's place?**

▶ 4. By Whose Standard?

Say: **Let's look at a few real-life people who have dealt with popularity, and see what they did.**

Form two groups, and assign each group one of these devotions and passages from *The Youth Bible*: "It's Not Who You Know ...," 1 Corinthians 3:1-23; or "Impressive!" Philip-pians 3:8-11. Have groups each read their story and the related scripture passage.

Distribute paper and pencils. Have groups work together to come up with a "Popularity Pact" that describes how they as a group will deal with popularity problems at school. When groups are finished, have them compare their pacts and create one overall pact for the whole group concerning popularity. Have someone with nice handwriting copy the pact onto poster-board. Then have a signing ceremony for all the kids in the group. Put the signed poster up on the wall.

Say: **Let's help each other avoid the popularity trap and remember that God is the one we really need to please.**

▶ 5. Song Prayer

Say: **Let's listen to a song by Steven Curtis Chapman, the singer one of our groups read about just a few minutes ago. The song is called "The Human Race." While you listen to it, pray silently for friends and other people you know who are caught up in the popularity game, that God will change their hearts.**

Play the song, encouraging kids to close their eyes as they pray.

To close, have kids sing "Change My Heart, Oh God" or "I Have Decided to Follow Jesus" from *The Group Songbook* (Group Books).

151

IN TOUCH WITH GOD

THEME: Prayer

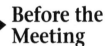

Before the Meeting

Gather a marker, newsprint, a portable radio/cassette player with headphones, pencils, 3×5 cards, photocopies of the "Master Prayer" handout and a globe or large world map. Make sure you have enough copies of *The Youth Bible* for each student to have one.

The toughest thing about prayer is actually doing it. In this meeting you'll help kids understand some things about the nature of prayer and encourage them to get started praying.

1. Anybody Listening?

Say: **I want to spend a few minutes taking the pulse of our group. Tell me what's going on that you like, what you'd like to see us change, and what new ideas we could try.**

Get a marker and newsprint ready to jot down ideas. Then turn on your cassette player and put on the headphones. As kids struggle to get you to hear what they are saying, jot down their names and leave a blank, write a question mark, or write any phrase that sounds similar to their words. (Naturally, those phrases may be somewhat humorous!) "Jive" to the music as the kids get louder and louder trying to communicate with you.

Take off the headphones and ask: **How did you feel trying to get me to hear and respond to you? How was this like or unlike trying to talk to God in prayer? When you pray, have you ever felt that nobody was really listening? How does that make you feel?**

Say: **Let's read a story about a man who kept on asking until he got what he wanted.**

Have a volunteer read Luke 11:1-13 aloud.

Then ask: **How do you feel when somebody interrupts your sleep? What do you think Jesus wants us to learn from this story? How would following Jesus' advice change your prayer life?**

Read aloud the accompanying devotion, "Countdown to Victory" and have kids answer the questions at the end.

2. A Hot Topic

Distribute pencils and 3×5 cards.

Say: **I don't want anyone to get nervous, but I'm going to give you a quiz. I'll ask questions; you'll write down percentages for answers.**

- **What percent of teenagers say they often pray for help when they have problems?**
- **What percent of teenagers say they often pray God will help other people?**
- **What percent of teenagers say they pray at least once a week outside church and other than before meals?**
- **What percent of teenagers say personal prayer is an important influence in their lives?**
- **What percent of teenagers say they are interested in learning how to pray?**

Have kids check their answers by turning to the devotion "Do You Have a Prayer?" (p. 1088 in *The Youth Bible*). An answer that falls within 10 percent of what was recorded in the survey will be counted correct. Have kids tell how many they got right.

Then ask: **What surprised you about this survey? How do these statistics make you feel? How important is learning about prayer to you, personally?**

3. Master Pray-er

Distribute photocopies of the "Master Prayer" handout.

Say: **The disciples expressed a desire to know about prayer. Jesus responded by teaching them what we know as "The Lord's Prayer."**

Ask a volunteer to read Luke 11:2-4 aloud. Then have kids work in pairs to complete the handout. Encourage them to look at this exercise as if Jesus were personally teaching them.

Bring everyone together and ask: **How did it feel to have Jesus himself teach you to pray? How would your life change if you followed this formula for prayer every day?**

4. The Best Policy

Read aloud "Praying About Real Life" (p. 312 in *The Youth Bible*).

Ask: **Have you ever had a similar experience to Shelley's? How did you deal with it? Is it okay to get angry with God—and let him know it? What happens when we are really honest with God in prayer?**

Say: **Honesty really is the best policy in prayer. God already knows how we feel. By admitting our feelings, we invite God to be part of the process of working through them.**

5. Cover the Globe

To close your meeting, read aloud the devotion "Pray for All People," along with 1 Timothy 2:1-4.

Set a globe or a large world map in front of your group. Explain that you want to cover the globe with prayer this week. Let kids volunteer to pray for specific countries or areas of the world. Give opportunities for kids to share what they know about the culture and concerns of their chosen places. Challenge kids to watch for items in the news that will help them pray knowledgeably for their area.

Then gather the group in a circle around the globe. Join hands and have kids pray for the area of the world they chose.

Master Prayer

Read Luke 11:2-4.

1. "Give us . . ."
List some of your needs:

List some of the needs of
another person you could
pray for:

2. "Forgive us . . . As we forgive . . ."
Write the initials of someone who sinned against you:

Have you forgiven this person?   Yes   No

Explain what your next step should be:

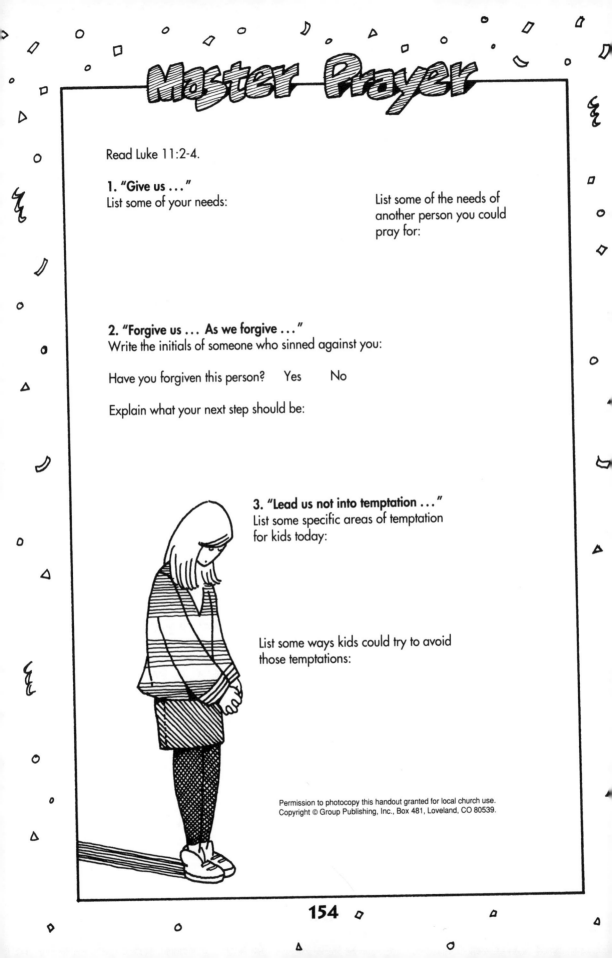

3. "Lead us not into temptation . . ."
List some specific areas of temptation
for kids today:

List some ways kids could try to avoid
those temptations:

WHO CARES?

THEME: Priorities

Before the Meeting

Gather 3×5 cards, pencils, paper, newsprint, several rolls of masking tape and fine-point markers. Make sure everyone has a copy of *The Youth Bible*.

What comes first in kids' lives? Too often what kids say comes first and what their lives say comes first aren't the same thing. This meeting challenges kids to scrutinize their lifestyles and encourages them to make their priorities the same as God's.

▶ 1. Looking Out for #1

As kids enter, give them each seven 3×5 cards and a pencil.

Say: **Think of the seven most important things in your life right now. You don't need to rank them. Just write a different one on each of your cards.**

When everyone is ready, have kids sit in a circle.

Say: **Presto Change-o! A nuclear war has just occurred, and life as we know it is forever changed. The things that are most important to us will soon be taken away— one by one. Every day for the next six days, you'll have to give up one of the things you hold most dear in life. But you must decide what to give up first, second, and so on.**

Okay, it's Day 1, and a tidal wave has just wiped out all the electricity in your town. You must give up one thing in your hand. What can you best afford to live without? Throw it on the floor.

Have kids throw one of their cards on the floor. Continue to count down the next five days, using these slightly silly and amazing catastrophes as reasons why kids have to give up their most important things: Day 2—Your dog begins to glow; Day 3—The water crawls out of the sink; Day 4—Your lawn hides the mower; Day 5—Acid rain dissolves your school; and Day 6—Jet fuel becomes strangely appetizing to you.

After kids throw down the next to the last card, ask: **What was hard about this activity? What surprised you about it? You have one card left in your hand. Is it what you thought it would be? If not, explain. What is the most important thing in your life?**

Most kids will probably respond by saying

"God," or "my relationship with God."

Say: **It's easy to *say* what our priorities are, but our true priorities come to light when we have to start giving things up.**

2. Put Your Time Where Your Card Is

Say: **Each of you holds a card that tells the most important thing in your life. Let's do a little quiz to see if your top priority shines out through your daily life.**

Give kids each a sheet of paper and say: **Down the left side of your paper, list the seven top priorities you wrote on your cards. Next to each one, "guesstimate" the number of hours you spend each week related to that priority. For example, if one of your priorities is "friends," then guesstimate how many hours you spend with friends each week.**

Have kids each complete their time chart, then ask volunteers to tell what they wrote.

Ask: **How does your top priority rate according to your time chart? What might this tell you about your priorities? How do you feel about what the time chart implies about your true priorities? Explain.**

Say: **Many people believe we spend our time on the things that are most important to us. Although that point can be debated, this activity still gives us reason to question what our true priorities might be.**

3. The Priority Word

Form four groups, and assign each group one of the following devotions and passages from *The Youth Bible*: "Worth a Sacrifice," Genesis 22:1-18; "Doing the Right Thing," Matthew 10:34-42; "What Are You Worth?" Matthew 22:1-14; or "Proms and Personalities," John 6:24-51. Have groups each read their devotion and scripture passage, then decide as a group what God's priorities are, based on the story and passage they read.

While kids work, tape a sheet of newsprint to the wall. When groups are ready, have them share their findings. Write their responses on the newsprint.

Ask: **How do the priorities we've listed here compare with your personal priorities? What can we do to make our personal priorities more like God's priorities?**

List kids' responses on newsprint.

4. Sticky Commitments

Toss out rolls of masking tape and fine-tip markers.

Say: **For our closing, let's make a commitment to pray for God to change our priorities to be more like his.**

Have kids each find a partner. Give each pair two strips of masking tape and a fine-tip marker.

Say: **On both strips of tape, write one of God's priorities listed on the newsprint that you want to begin building into your lifestyle. Tape one strip in the front cover of your *Youth Bible*, and give the other strip to your partner to tape in his or her *Youth Bible*. Then pray for each other, asking God's help in building these new priorities into your lives.**

If kids don't own Bibles, have them tape their strips to their clothes and take them home to put on their bedroom wall.

PROMISES THAT LAST

THEME: Promises

> Cross my heart and hope to die, stick a needle in my eye.
>   That's how some kids affirm their promises. But teenagers recognize that making and keeping promises is more complicated than just repeating a cute phrase. This meeting encourages young people to seriously consider the promises of God, who, unlike people, is never deceptive and will not lie.

▶ Before the Meeting

If possible, obtain a recording of one of the songs listed in activity 1 and a portable stereo. Write the questions listed in activity 3 on separate 3×5 cards, along with any questions you'd like to add. Gather two suitcases, markers, stick-on nametags, potholders and a dish. Make sure everyone has a copy of *The Youth Bible*.

▶ 1. Name That Tune

Form four groups, and secretly assign each group one of these oldies tunes: "Will You Love Me Tomorrow?" "Runaway," "Peggy Sue," and "Hang on Sloopy." Inform all the groups that they've been given an oldies song title. Tell each group they must perform a group charade to try to get the other groups to guess its song. Give groups a few minutes to prepare, then have them each present their charade. Praise kids' efforts, then announce the song titles if they weren't all guessed.

Ask: **What relationship issue do you think all these songs have in common?** Allow kids to guess, but realize that many of the kids won't be familiar with the songs.

Play a recording of one of the songs and ask the question again.

Then say: **All these songs, in one way or another, are talking about promises. People often break their promises, don't they? These songs point that out. But during this meeting, we'll examine some promises that you can rely on.**

▶ 2. Home on the Range

Read aloud the devotion "Trusting the Pilot" (p. 18 in *The Youth Bible*). Read only the first five paragraphs.

Then say: **Imagine how it would feel to be out in the middle of Africa with only a promise to sustain you. How would you** feel every time you heard an animal?

Select two people to play David and Gene. Provide luggage for them to sit on. Give half of the remaining kids each a nametag and a marker, and have them designate themselves as any dangerous wild animal they choose. (Tell the other half of the group that you'll give them another task later on.) Ask the "wild animals" to prowl around close to David and Gene, quietly making the appropriate noises.

After a minute or so, have kids freeze, then sit down where they are.

Say: **None of us is really stuck in Africa, but we're all in tough situations of one kind or another. What kinds of "wild animals" threaten you as you attempt to live a Christian life?**

Write kids' responses each on a separate nametag, then hand them out to the "wild animals" for them to stick on next to their animal nametag. Continue until all the animals have received new identities.

Then say: **Fortunately, we are not alone. Just like David and Gene, we have a fence to protect us.**

▶ 3. Safety Zone

Choose volunteers to read aloud Genesis 17: 1-10, Jeremiah 31:27-37 and the devotion "Changing Lives" (p. 727 in *The Youth Bible*). After the devotion and passages are read, have kids name the promises that are contained in them.

Record the promises on separate nametags, and give one of these new nametags to each of the remaining untagged kids. Have the "wild animals" back away from David and Gene. Then install the new kids as "fenceposts" around David and Gene. Have the fenceposts lock arms to keep the animals out.

When everyone is in place, have the wild animals try to touch David or Gene by trying to get through the protective "fence."

After allowing the animals several tries, stop the activity and ask: **How would you feel if**

you were David and Gene in this activity? What does this activity tell you about God's promises? How do we build these promises into our lives, so we can have a "fence" around us like David and Gene have?

Say: **The way we build God's promises into our lives is simple—we believe them. But believing in God's promises isn't always easy. Let's look at some reasons why people often fail to believe in God's promises.**

▶ 4. Hot Questions

Using potholders, hold on to a dish full of the questions you wrote down before the meeting and say: **Here are a few "hot" questions that help us understand why we might fail to believe in God's promises.**

Invite volunteers to come forward and draw one question from the dish. Have the volunteer read aloud the question, then allow him or her 20 seconds to think about it before responding. Once the person has responded, allow the group to discuss the question as well.

Here are some sample questions (feel free to add your own):

- Does trusting God's promises mean that we'll never feel pain?
- How long does it take God to "make good" on a promise?
- Can God ever take back a promise?
- Do God's promises have conditions attached to them?
- If God's promises are designed to protect us, why does he still allow bad things to happen to us?

After the discussion, say: **Some of these difficult issues just come down to a matter of trust. God is wiser than we are. Sometimes we don't understand why he allows things to happen. But even if we don't understand—especially when we don't understand—we can still believe that he's working things out for the best.**

158

5. Partner Beatitudes

Lead the group in the first "Consider ..." activity in the devotion "Changing Lives" (p. 727 in *The Youth Bible*).

Have kids find partners and open their Bibles to Matthew 5:1-12.

Have kids each read this section of scripture aloud to their partner, using their partner's name to begin each verse.

Bring everyone together and close with prayer, thanking God for his promises and asking help for kids to trust them.

PRODIGAL PEOPLE

THEME: Rebellion

People don't always agree about whether teenage rebellion is sometimes okay or always wrong. But everyone agrees that when rebellion goes too far, it's ultimately the teenagers who pay—sometimes even with their lives.

How can you impress on kids the dangers of living with a rebellious attitude? This meeting helps kids experience what happens when rebellion goes too far—and gives them hope for reversing rebellious attitudes.

▶ Before the Meeting

Find a location for your meeting that you can make completely "light tight"—so that no light leaks through. Cover windows with blankets or black plastic (or both) and tape the light switches in the "off" position. Gather newsprint, tape, markers, flashlight, pencils and two photocopies of the handout for each person. Make sure everyone has a copy of *The Youth Bible*.

▶ 1. Inside My Head

Before kids arrive, shut the doors of the meeting room and tape a sheet of newsprint to a wall outside the doors. As kids arrive, have them work in pairs to trace their partner's head on the newsprint with marker. Inside their head shapes, have kids each write things that happened this week that made them want to rebel.

When everyone is finished, have volunteers tell what they wrote, then ask: **Why is rebellion** so attractive sometimes? What's the best possible thing that could happen in your work, in your school or in your home if you totally rebelled? What's the worst possible thing that could happen?

Say: **Today we're going to talk about the consequences of rebellion. To start our meeting, we're going to enter the room a little differently than we usually do.**

Have kids enter the dark room one by one on their hands and knees. Tell them to find a seat and wait for the rest of the group to enter.

Once everyone is inside, walk in with a flashlight, close the door and ask: **How did it feel to find your way in the dark? How is that like living a rebellious lifestyle?**

Say: **Rebellion can cut us off from people who help guide us in life. It can even cut us off from God. Then we end up feeling like we're crawling around in the dark. Let's take a look at a couple of real-life situations involving rebellion.**

2. The Life of a Rebel

Have a volunteer use a flashlight to read the devotion "I'm Outta Here ..." (p. 1036 in *The Youth Bible*). Then read aloud the story of the prodigal son in Luke 15:11-32.

After the readings, ask: **What similarities and differences do you see between Liz's story and the one Jesus told? How were Liz and the younger son living life "in the dark"?**

Turn off the flashlight and ask: **How do you feel when the lights go out in your own life—when you totally cut yourself off from those who could guide and help you? How is your ability to function affected by living in the dark?**

3. Shapes in the Night

With the lights still off, give kids each a photocopy of the "You've Come a Long Way, Baby Doll" handout and instruct kids each to carefully tear out a paper doll of themselves. When everyone is finished, turn on the lights and ask: **How many of you were able to correctly tear out the shape on your paper? How many of you accidentally tore off an arm or a leg? How is this experience like what happens to you when you try to shape your life on your own through rebellion?**

Say: **When we try to "go it alone" by rebelling against our parents, teachers or church leaders, it's like trying to tear out a shape when you can't see the lines. Something almost always gets torn away. Then there are unpleasant consequences. Let's look at what happened to a guy named Mitch.**

Have volunteers read aloud the devotion "This Is My Life" (p. 403 in *The Youth Bible*) and the related scripture passage, 2 Chronicles 24:17-25. Discuss the first question at the end of the devotion.

Then ask: **What were the consequences of Joash's rebellion? of Mitch's?**

Say: **Let's see how we can turn our lives away from rebellion and avoid living in the dark.**

4. Diary Rewrite

Distribute pencils and have kids turn to "Donna's Diary" (p. 293 in *The Youth Bible*). On their paper dolls, have kids each rewrite Donna's story, changing it so that this time Donna makes good decisions instead of bad ones. When everyone is finished, have volunteers read aloud what they wrote.

Then ask: **How do we avoid rebellion?**

Remind kids of the newsprint they wrote on outside the room and ask: **In those situations you listed outside, how can you avoid rebellion?**

After several kids respond, say: **In any situation that tempts you to rebel, you have to choose how you're going to respond. By making wise choices, you can avoid rebellion and stay out of the "dark" in life.**

 ## 5. You've Come a Long Way, Baby Doll

Give kids each a fresh photocopy of the "You've Come a Long Way, Baby Doll" handout and have them tear it out—this time with the lights on.

Have kids each turn to 1 John 1:7 in *The Youth Bible* and copy the verse onto their doll. Encourage kids to take their dolls home and put them up as a reminder to avoid rebellion and stay "in the light" of God's guidance.

Close with prayer, asking God to help kids walk in his light and avoid rebellion at home, at work and at school.

You've Come a Long Way, Baby Doll

GET MAD, GET EVEN OR GET OVER IT?

THEME: Revenge

Go ahead. Make my day.
Those famous words reflect a popular opinion held by many people today. If you try to hurt me, I'll hurt you back. Actually, it's not a new outlook on life at all. For as far back as records were kept, people were hurting and killing others in the name of revenge.

But God has some different ideas about revenge—ideas that blatantly clash with mainstream culture. This meeting challenges kids' opinions about revenge and helps them learn how to receive God's grace to "get over it" rather than to "get even."

▶ Before the Meeting

Bring a large stack of old newspapers to the meeting room. Gather stick-on name-tags, slips of paper, pencils, marker, newsprint and masking tape. Make sure everyone has a copy of *The Youth Bible*.

▶ 1. Silly Soap

As kids arrive, give them each a blank nametag, a slip of paper and a pencil. Form a circle and have kids number off. Then have kids each write their number on their nametag and their slip of paper. Collect the slips of paper, shuffle them and redistribute them to the group. Make sure no one gets his or her own number. Tell kids not to reveal the numbers on their slips of paper.

Have kids put on their nametags and say: **You are all now part of the cast of the new soap opera,** *Days of Our Livers.* **In the scene you're all about to perform, you are at a party in a great ballroom in Bermuda. But,** alas, there is malice in the air, for the person whose number you hold has done a rotten thing to you which is too horrible to mention, and now you must get revenge. The method of revenge you choose is up to you—you can shoot, stab or bludgeon your enemy until he or she is dead.

There are only two rules:
1. Whatever weapon you use must be formed out of newspapers.
2. Only your weapon may touch your target—you cannot make any direct

physical contact.

Direct kids each to the stack of newspapers and allow them each a few minutes to create their weapons. Then call everyone to the center of the room.

Just before starting the scene, say: **The object of the scene is to get revenge on your enemy before someone else gets revenge on you.** Once kids are struck, have them sit down.

After the scene, ask: **How did it feel to get revenge on your enemy? How did it feel knowing someone you didn't know was trying to get revenge on you? How would life be different if everyone were always trying to get back at each other this way?**

▶ 2. Paper Stoning

Say: **Revenge has been a way of life for some people ever since time began. But a few people in history went against the norm. Let's re-create one of the most classic examples of someone who chose not to take revenge on his enemies.**

Have a volunteer read aloud Acts 7:51-60. After the reading, assign one of the kids to be "Stephen" and have the rest of the kids shape their paper weapons into paper "stones." Read through the story again, this time having kids act it out as you read it.

After the stoning, ask: **How did it feel to stone "Stephen"? How did it feel when Stephen did nothing to retaliate? Based on this experience, what's the best way to respond when someone attacks you at school, at work or at home? Explain.**

▶ 3. Another Way

Say: **Let's look at some situations and scriptures that may give us clues for other alternatives to revenge.**

Form three groups. Assign each group one of the following devotions and passages from *The Youth Bible*: "A Violent Cycle," Genesis 45:3-8; "Hate Stealer," Psalm 17; and "Different Strength," Isaiah 50:4-9.

Have groups each read their devotion and passage, then brainstorm alternatives to revenge when faced with a hurtful situation. After a few minutes, have groups each tell what they came up with. Record their responses on newsprint.

Say: **God wants us to take potentially hurtful situations and use them as opportunities to build bridges between people. We can begin to do this by not taking revenge when other people hurt us.**

▶ 4. Paper Bridges

Form pairs and give each pair a roll of masking tape. Collect the balled up newspapers and have kids make more balls from the stack of newspapers you brought.

Say: **Using the newspaper balls and the masking tape, work with your partner to create a bridge that we'll call "the bridge of no revenge."**

Encourage kids to be creative in their bridge design. When pairs are finished, line the bridges along the walls of the meeting room and praise kids' work. Tell them you'll keep the bridges where they are for several weeks as a reminder to build bridges rather than throw stones when others hurt them.

Close with prayer, asking God to help kids not to take revenge when others hurt them.

THE BLUES

THEME: Sadness

Am I blue? Am I blue? Ain't these tears in my eyes tellin' you? While those may be the lyrics to an old tune, they are the message behind much of what young people today are singing, saying and feeling. With constant crises on international, national, family and personal levels, teenagers must grow a faith that will help them deal with inevitable sadness. This meeting will explore stories of sadness in the lives of young people and relate them to scriptural passages that point toward health and wholeness.

 Before the Meeting

You'll need posterboard, a marker, shoe boxes, pencils and paper. Make sure everyone has a copy of *The Youth Bible*.

▶ 1. How Sad Would YOU Be?

Place a poster with a 1 on it at one end of the room and a poster with a 10 on it at the opposite end. Tell the group that for the next few moments you'll be taking a survey about what makes them feel sad.

Say: **I'll be giving you a few situations that might be upsetting to some people. If I give you one that would make you feel very sad, stand close to the 10. If this particular event wouldn't bother you too much, stand closer to the 1.**

Tell kids to be prepared to discuss why they respond the way they do. Read aloud these situations:

- **You wake up one morning to find that due to weather conditions, your school has been closed for the day.**
- **You discover that last year's science teacher is passing out photocopies of your old lab reports—as examples of how NOT to do it.**
- **Your best friend goes out with your boyfriend (girlfriend) the day after you break up.**
- **Your vacation to Europe is cancelled because of money problems.**
- **Your dad loses his job.**
- **Your aunt dies suddenly of a heart attack.**
- **You don't get a date for the prom.**
- **You discover that a good friend of yours has an alcohol problem.**

At various points during the activity, ask specific young people why they're standing where they are. Encourage kids to freely discuss the types of sadness involved in any of these situations, as well as the other emotions that might be present.

Ask: **Did you ever feel sad or alone because you were the only one standing in a particular spot? Explain. How is that like the feelings people have when these things happen to them in real life?**

Conclude this activity by saying that each day we're all faced with situations that could radically affect how we feel. Explain that one reason the church has been strong over the years is that Christians have banded together in times of joy and sadness and helped each other rely on their faith in God.

 ## 2. A Small Circle of Friends

Form three groups of two to five. Assign each group one of the following devotions and passages from *The Youth Bible*: "Death Watch," Ecclesiastes 3:1-13; "Stabbed in the Back," Zechariah 12:7-10; or "The Worst Year of Her Life," Revelation 7:9-17.

Say: **Each of these devotions features a story about a person who was feeling sad: Derek, Denise and Lexie all went through tough times. Find out as much as you can about these people and try to discover how they might have felt. Put yourself in their shoes and uncover some of the emotions that they must have been experiencing.**

After groups have familiarized themselves with their characters, have them each read the scripture passage accompanying their devotion and discuss how that passage might be helpful to someone in their character's situation. Then bring everyone together and have groups summarize their stories and the helpful ideas from scripture.

3. Have Kit, Will Travel

Have a volunteer read aloud the four statistics at the beginning of the devotion "Chasing the Blues Away" (p. 681 in *The Youth Bible*). Ask kids to think about people they know who might be in such situations.

Ask: **How would someone who was feeling this way find help in our group?**

Ask another person to read aloud Isaiah 61:1-11 and brainstorm ways your group can help fulfill the prophecy given in those verses.

Give each group a shoe box, a pencil and paper. Have groups each brainstorm and write down what they would put in a "Smile-Aid Kit" that would help people deal with sadness. For example: kids could include tissue, each member's phone number, an 800 number from a help hotline, scripture passages, and jokes or cartoons.

Bring everyone together and have groups share the "contents" of their Smile-Aid Kits. Challenge kids to bring some of the items they listed to your next meeting.

4. Letter to a Friend

Form pairs. Give each person a pencil and a sheet of paper. Have the kids read the devotion "Does Anybody Care?" (p. 960 in *The Youth Bible*).

Say: **Let's take time to practice what we've learned. Pretend that Joyce and Louise go to your school and are acquaintances (not close friends) of yours. In your pairs, one of you write a letter to Joyce (offering support), and the other write a letter to Louise (offering her advice on how to be a friend to Joyce). Get ideas for your letters from the "Consider . . . " activities from the devotions we've looked at today.**

After a few minutes, have partners read their letters to each other. Then have partners pray together for people they know who are sad.

5. Circle of Support

Gather kids in a circle. Ask if anyone would like special prayer for feelings of sadness they have right now. Also ask kids to mention first names of friends who are going through a period of sadness.

Close with a time of prayer for these people. Thank God for the encouragement he offers in scripture for the sad times we will all face.

BORED OF EDUCATION?

THEME: School

While some students may admit to enjoying school, most will say their favorite subject is lunch. Some kids feel school is boring and irrelevant; others find it stressful and pressured-filled. There is pressure from teachers to study, from parents to bring home good grades, from peers to conform. Christian students also feel the pressure to take a stand for Christ. This meeting will help students see some of the benefits of education and encourage them to view God as a source of strength, *not* pressure.

▶ Before the Meeting

Gather four candy bars (or other small prizes), four blindfolds, paper, pencils and 3×5 cards. As an option for activity 3, bring a cassette player and a tape of a popular rap song. Make sure everyone has a copy of *The Youth Bible*.

▶ 1. Help or Hinder?

Ask four volunteers to leave the room. Hide the candy bars in the room, letting all of the remaining kids see where they are. Divide these kids into two groups, instructing one group to be helpers and the other to be hinderers. Have kids stand, sit and lie about the room to create some obstacles.

Blindfold the four volunteers and bring them back into the room.

Say: **There are candy bars hidden in this room that you can find and eat. In order to find them, listen to the voices of the other students who will be shouting out instructions. They will not touch you or move around; they'll just direct you with their voices. The only problem is that some will be telling you the truth and some will be giving you false information. There is no way for you to tell which are helping or hindering—you just have to choose which voices you will follow.**

Let the blindfolded kids search while the others direct them. If the searchers find a candy bar they can take off their blindfolds and eat the candy. After several minutes of searching and shouting, call an end to the activity and bring everyone together. Thank the volunteers and give them any unfound candy bars as a reward for being willing to participate.

Ask volunteers: **How did you decide which voices to follow? Did those voices help you or not? What other situations have you faced in life (especially in school) that seemed confusing?**

Ask helpers: **How did it feel to be able to help the volunteers? How did it feel when they wouldn't listen to you? What kinds of "advice givers" do you encounter at school? How might their feelings be like and unlike the ones you've just experienced?**

Ask hinderers: **How did you feel leading the volunteers astray? Did you ever wish you could have helped them instead? In your opinion, why do some kids try to lead others down the wrong road?**

Say: **During our lives there are many "voices" that try to instruct us. Right now you probably hear a lot of those voices at school—everyone seems to be telling you what to do. Choosing which voices to follow and which to avoid is often confusing. In this meeting we're going to see how the Bible can help us.**

▶ 2. Wise Lectures

Form three groups. Assign each group one of the following devotions and passages from *The Youth Bible*: "Stunned Into Action," Proverbs 2:1-10; "Crossroads," Proverbs 9:8-12; or "The Powerful Way," 1 Corinthians 2:1-11.

Have kids read their devotions and passages and discuss the questions at the end. Explain that each group should tell what their character's problem with school was, how they handled it, and what helpful advice their scripture passage offered.

Allow a few minutes for groups to study and prepare their presentations. Then bring everyone together and have groups share their findings.

Ask: **How do we get wisdom, according to the Bible? What are some of the rewards of wisdom? How do these rewards relate to school? What makes it hard for you, personally, to seek wisdom at school?**

▶ 3. Rappin'

Have students return to their groups. Distribute paper and pencils. Ask kids to read the "For More, See ..." passages in their devotions and then make up a rap song based on the passages about how God helps us and rewards us at school. (As an option, you could play a popular rap song on cassette to get imaginations flowing.)

Invite each group to perform its rap for the rest of the kids.

▶ 4. Personalizing Verses

Say: **You all have discovered that God wants us to learn and rewards us for that. God wants to help us, not hinder us. He will help us choose what is best.**

Distribute 3×5 cards. Have kids look at the first "Consider ..." option in the devotion "Stunned Into Action" (p. 569) that suggests writing encouraging verses in their school notebooks.

Say: **I'd like each of you to find a verse that will encourage you at school. Write it on one of your cards and transfer it to a school notebook later. This will help remind you that God is behind you and can help you make it through school.**

HOW MUCH AM I WORTH?

THEME: Self-Esteem

Teenagers get mixed messages about what really gives them value. The world tells them true worth comes from what they have or achieve. But God's unconditional love is what really builds kids' self-esteem. Use this meeting to help kids see their value to God.

Before the Meeting

You'll need newsprint, crayons or markers, tape, paper, pencils, 3×5 cards and construction paper. Make sure everyone has a copy of *The Youth Bible*.

▶ 1. Try Tracing

Have kids form pairs. Give each person a human-size sheet of newsprint and a crayon or marker. Tell partners to take turns lying on the paper while the other partner traces a body outline with the crayon. Kids can lie in any "weird" position they desire.

After kids have finished the outlines, have them each personalize their outline by drawing in symbols. Write these instructions on newsprint:

1. Head: draw a symbol for your favorite subject in school
2. Heart: draw a symbol for your most treas-ured personality trait
3. Hand: draw a symbol for something you do well
4. Foot: draw a symbol for a way you help others
5. Around the outside of the outline: draw pictures of your most important possessions

Have kids each tape their labeled body outlines to the wall.

Then form a circle and ask: **What do these body outlines tell us about people? How easy or difficult was it to think of symbols for your outline? Which says more about who you are—the internal or external things on your outline? Which has the greatest influence on how you feel about yourself?**

▶ 2. What Matters?

Form seven groups (a group can be just one person). Give each group member a sheet of paper, a pencil and a 3×5 card with one of these passages and devotions from *The Youth Bible* written on it: 1 Samuel 16:1-13 and "Bigger Isn't Always Better"; Psalm 8 and "A Speck?"; Jeremiah 1:4-10 and "The New Kid in the Group"; Amos 6:1-7 and "It's What's Inside"; Matthew 10:24-33 and "Playing Your Part"; Luke 19:1-10 and "Geek in Glasses"; and 1 Peter 2:2-10 and "Paying the Price."

Have groups each read through their devotion and passage. Explain that you're going to ask several questions. Groups will discuss each question and report their answers to the rest of the class.

The questions are: **What external factor did people in this passage or devotion look to for self-esteem? How did God view that external factor? What internal factor did God value?**

Say: **Our society values external factors such as wealth, power and beauty. But these things are fleeting. People can lose all their money, be thrown out of public office or be disfigured in an accident. True self-esteem comes from what can never be taken away; it comes from the valuable qualities in each of us.**

Ask: **Based on your reading of these passages, would you say our relationship with God is based more on internal or external factors? How can we keep our self-esteem linked to God's view of us rather than the other things that often seem so important, such as looks, possessions, money, power, status or position?**

▶ 3. Face Yourself

Have kids sit in a circle. Ask for three volunteers to be the narrator, Susan and Gina in the devotion "Be Yourself" (p. 1183 of *The Youth Bible*). Have them each read their appropriate parts in the devotion.

Then read aloud 1 Corinthians 12:1-11. Ask the two questions in the devotion. After some discussion, give a sheet of construction paper and a crayon to each person.

Say: **Draw your own face but don't let anyone see what you are doing. When you're done, fold the paper and put it in the center of the circle with the others.**

When the "faces" are all in a pile, shuffle them. Have kids each pick one and tape it to what they think is the matching body outline on the wall. Have kids each tell if their face was matched correctly with their body and rearrange faces that weren't matched correctly.

Gather kids in a circle. Have kids each tell one gift or positive quality they see in the person on their left.

Say: **How does hearing good things about ourselves promote better self-esteem? Is this something we can (or should) be doing for each other on a regular basis? Explain.**

▶ 4. Remembering Your Family Ties

Give kids the quiz from the devotion "Are You Okay?" (p. 661 in *The Youth Bible*). Ask for volunteers to respond to each situation. Point out that our self-esteem as God's children is directly related to God's greatness. In spite of circumstances in our lives, God remains in total control, and he deeply loves us.

Tell kids to think about that as you read aloud Isaiah 44:1-8. Close by thanking God for giving us worth and dignity. Ask God to help kids base their self-esteem on his love rather than outward qualities.

SERVING ISN'T FOR COWARDS

THEME: Service (1)

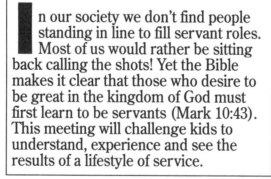

In our society we don't find people standing in line to fill servant roles. Most of us would rather be sitting back calling the shots! Yet the Bible makes it clear that those who desire to be great in the kingdom of God must first learn to be servants (Mark 10:43). This meeting will challenge kids to understand, experience and see the results of a lifestyle of service.

▶ **Before the Meeting**

You'll need a marker, newsprint, tape, peel-off stickers, cleaning supplies, 3×5 cards and pencils. Make arrangements with the custodial staff of your church for kids to clean the church bathrooms. Have a copy of *The Youth Bible* for each person.

▶ **1. Signs of Fear**

Write the following 10 things that people fear on separate sheets of newsprint: jumping out of a plane, giving a speech to 500 people, failing a test, eating something gross, walking barefoot through a snakepit, being covered with bugs, crossing a cemetery at night, asking someone out for a date, being trapped in an elevator, never being able to eat chocolate again.

Tape the 10 signs to your meeting room walls. Give each person three peel-off stickers. Have kids put their stickers on the three things they fear the most. When kids have placed their stickers, total the number of stickers on each sign to determine your group's top three fears.

▶ **2. All-Star Servants**

Say: **As you can see, we share a lot of common fears. But many of us share a fear you may never have thought about.**

Ask: **How would you feel about always being the one to do dishes at your house? always cleaning the bathrooms? always jumping up to fetch things for others? Would you agree that many people are afraid of serving others? Why would someone be afraid to be a servant?**

Form three groups. Assign each group two of the following devotions and passages from *The Youth Bible*: "Gift for a Stranger," Genesis 18:1-16; "When People Can't Say Thanks," 1 Samuel 16:14-23; "Not Just Lip Service," Micah 6:1-8; "Volunteer of the Year," Mark 10:35-45; "The Lowly Star," John 13:1-17; and "When You See

It," Hebrews 13:1-8.

Have groups each read their devotions and passages, discuss the questions at the end, and come up with a definition of servanthood. Then bring everyone together and have kids share their definitions and tell what makes the characters in their devotions all-star servants.

 ## 3. I Can Serve

Say: **We are going to do something more scary than anything written on the signs here. We are going to practice being servants. We are going to clean the church bathrooms. If we all work together, we should be able to do in just a few minutes what could take an hour or more for the church custodian.**

Form separate groups of guys and girls. Appoint a leader for each group, assign individual members specific responsibilities in the cleaning, and pass out supplies.

Have a contest to see which group can be the first to have its bathroom spotless. Proclaim both groups winners for serving in this way.

Then ask: **How did you feel while you cleaned the bathroom? How did you respond when you were asked to do something? Who showed the most servant-like attitude in your group? Explain. How will the custodian feel when he or she comes to work tomorrow and finds the bathrooms spotless? How do you think God feels about your work in the bathrooms?**

4. Servant Motivation

Ask volunteers to read aloud the devotion "Are You Jesus?" (p. 955 in *The Youth Bible*) and the related scripture passage, Matthew 25:31-46.

Ask: **How does the child's question make you feel? How do you think that response will affect Eric's life? Explain.**

Then discuss the questions at the end of the devotion.

Distribute 3×5 cards and pencils, and lead kids in the first "Consider ..." activity. Have them each write down the name of someone they see each day and how they can serve that person.

Close by praying that God will help kids each be a servant—even when they get treated like one!

LIFE ON THE LINE

THEME: Service (2)

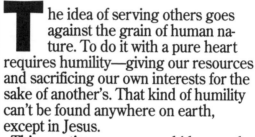

The idea of serving others goes against the grain of human nature. To do it with a pure heart requires humility—giving our resources and sacrificing our own interests for the sake of another's. That kind of humility can't be found anywhere on earth, except in Jesus.

This meeting encourages kids to evaluate themselves as servants and to plug into the power of Christ to serve others.

▶ Before the Meeting

Tape a large sheet of newsprint to the wall. Title it "Service Contract," and under the title, write "I choose to commit my life to serving God by serving others." Gather pencils, 3×5 cards, markers and tape. Make sure everyone has a copy of *The Youth Bible*.

be able to contribute something to help your team win?

Say: **In life, like in this game, we all have different things we can contribute. At some time or other we need to ask ourselves, "What will I do with what I've been given?" Let's see how some people have answered that question in their lives.**

▶ 1. Scavengers

Form two teams and have teams race to bring you each of the items listed below. Name one item at a time and don't allow kids to leave the room to find them. Here are the items: five sneakers, three belts, four rings, five purses, 37 pennies, 7 earrings, 6 things that are red, a pack of gum, a drivers license.

After the game, congratulate the winning team, then ask: **What did it take to win this game? Was there any one person who had everything I asked for? How did it feel to**

▶ 2. Servant Examples

Form three groups. Assign each group two of the following devotions and passages from *The Youth Bible*: "Called to Compassion," Isaiah 42:1-9; "Life on the Altar," John 12:1-11; "Worthy of the Trust," 1 Corinthians 4:1-5; "Doing What We Can," 2 Corinthians 5:20—6:10; "Free to Serve," Galatians 5:13-26; and "Thanks for Coming," 3 John 5-8.

Have groups each read aloud their devotions and passages, then discuss the questions at the end.

Then bring everyone together and ask: **How are the people in these stories alike? What are they doing with the gifts God has given them? According to the verses we've heard, how would you summarize God's view of servanthood?**

 ## 3. Never Give Up

Ask a volunteer to read aloud the devotion "Sweating on a Shingle" (p. 1023 in *The Youth Bible*).

Pause before the discussion questions and ask: **Why did everyone want to give up on the project? What turned things around for them so they were motivated to keep working? When have you been tempted to give up on a service project? What did it feel like to hang in there and finish?**

Have a second volunteer read aloud the related scripture passage, Luke 10:25-37. Then discuss the questions at the end of the devotion.

4. It's My Turn

Say: **Now that we've seen how others have used their abilities to serve God, let's turn the spotlight onto ourselves.**

Distribute 3×5 cards and pencils. Have kids each write on their card three or four of their talents or abilities—but not their name. When kids are finished, collect the cards.

After shuffling the cards, read them aloud one by one and have kids brainstorm ways each talent or ability could be used for God at church, at school, or elsewhere in the world. After discussing all the cards, pass the stack around and have kids each retrieve their card.

Say: **Now that we have some ideas for ways we can use our special talents to serve God, let's go the next step and commit to starting to serve more this week.**

5. Service Contract

Show the group the Service Contract and read it aloud.

Then say: **There are lots of ways to demonstrate your commitment to serve others. But today we can do it by simply taping our cards to this contract and signing it. This will be a symbol of our determination to find new ways to serve God—starting this week.**

Provide tape and markers. On their cards, have kids each put a star by (or write out) one specific way they'll use their talents in God's service. Then have them each sign their card and tape it to the contract.

When everyone is finished, close with prayer, asking God to help kids understand and live out their new servant lifestyle.

HOW FAR IS TOO FAR?

THEME: Sexuality

In a recent survey, 43 percent of conservative Christian 18-year-olds said they have had premarital sexual intercourse. These are the kids in our churches and youth groups. Almost half of them have had sex outside of marriage before the age of "adulthood." Kids need to see that God has good reasons for wanting us to save sex for marriage—reasons that are good for us, not just for him.

Use this session to help kids see that they can resist having sex and that eventually they'll be glad they waited. This session will also help kids remember that God loves them and will forgive them no matter how badly they've messed up.

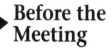

Before the Meeting

Gather enough chocolate kisses and business-size cards for everyone to have one. Also gather a bucket of warm, soapy water, a towel, paper and pencils. Be sure you have available a chalkboard and chalk, or newsprint and a marker. Have a copy of *The Youth Bible* for each person.

1. The Trouble With Sex

Read aloud the devotion "Once Forgiven, What Then?" (p. 1071 in *The Youth Bible*).

Say: **Stephanie and Ross had a problem with sex. Their passion got the best of them, even when they both had good intentions. It's a problem lots of kids have today—even Christian kids. And sex isn't** easy to resist sometimes. **In this meeting we're going to take a look at how the Bible teaches us to deal with sexual desire.**

2. Sticky Situations

Distribute chocolate kisses. Have kids each unwrap their kisses and hold them in their hands until you give the word that it's okay to eat them.

Have each person in your group tell their favorite candy. If kids try to eat their kisses or even lick their chocolaty hands, scold them for it and remind them that they need to wait. Continue the discussion until every kiss has left a chocolate mess in its owner's hand.

Ask: **How hard was it to resist licking the chocolate from your hands and eating the** kisses? How is that like how hard it can be to control our physical desires? What would have made the candy easier to resist? Keeping it in the wrapper? Leaving it on a table? Leaving the bag unopened? How is this similiar to ways we can think of to avoid giving in to our natural sexual desires?

Let kids eat their chocolates, then wash off their hands in the bucket of water.

Say: **We've played a game with chocolate kisses today—but real kisses are nothing to play with. We need to understand our passions and learn to control them or any of us could end up sorry like Stephanie and Ross. Let's look at some other kids' experiences and Bible passages to help us learn to make good decisions about sex.**

▶ 3. Sex and Consequences

Form two groups. Assign each group two of the following devotions and passages from *The Youth Bible*: "Risking Everything," 2 Samuel 11:1-15; "How Far?" Song of Solomon 5:2-6; "A Special Gift," Matthew 5:27-37; and "It Could Happen to Me," 1 Corinthians 10:1-13.

Give each group paper and a pencil. Have both groups read their devotions and passages. Tell group 1 to list what the people in the story and passage did that led them into problems with sex. Tell group 2 to list what the people in the story and passage did that kept them out of problems. When groups are ready, have them report.

Then ask: **What can we learn from these passages and stories to help us in handling our own desires?**

Write kids ideas on a chalkboard or newsprint as they list them. Keep prodding them until you get at least six ideas.

▶ 4. Love and Passion

Have kids read 1 Corinthians 13:4-8a. Form groups of three or four and have each group come up with a paraphrase of the passage based on "passion" instead of love. If you're

short on time, you might want to just read this example paraphrase while kids follow the real version in their Bibles.

Passion Paraphrase of 1 Corinthians 13:4-8a:

Passion is impatient; passion is unkind. It envies, it boasts, it is proud of its conquests. It is rude, self-seeking, easily angered, and keeps track of what is owed. Passion often rejoices in evil and doesn't like the truth. It always looks out for itself, never trusts, never thinks of the future, and usually burns out in a short time. Passion often disappoints.

Ask: **What are the differences between sexual desire and love?**

After kids have suggested several differences, move on to the closing activity.

▶ 5. Whiter Than Snow

Say: **Let's look at one more story and devotion.**

Have volunteers read aloud the devotion "Whiter Than Snow" and the related scripture passage, Psalm 51.

Say: **Even a great man of God like King David messed up sexually. And this psalm is his prayer of repentance. God's plan for us is to save sex for its proper, beautiful expression in marriage, but he's there to forgive us if we've made mistakes. And he wants us to return to him to be cleansed and to make a new commitment to remain true to him.**

Be sensitive to your kids at this point. If you think a group prayer seeking God's forgiveness is appropriate, this would be a good time for it.

Say: **To help us keep strong in our commitment to save sex for marriage, let's think right now about the limit of how far we'll go when the passion starts rising. The Bible doesn't give us specific guidelines about how far is too far, but let's keep in mind our exercise with the candy kisses. The closer you get, the harder it is to resist.**

Pass out cards (business-card size) and have

kids each privately write on their card how far they'll go when things begin to heat up. Encourage kids to keep the cards in their wallets and look at them as a reminder before every date. You might also want to have them write the words of 1 Corinthians 10:13 on the other side of the card.

Close your session with prayer, asking God to help your kids make wise decisions as they seek to save God's gift of sex for marriage.

SPEAK OUT!

THEME: Sharing Faith

Telling others about their faith is devastatingly difficult for most teenagers. Fear of rejection can stifle a truckload of good intentions. Kids need to see that faith-sharing is the believer's natural response to others' needs. This session will help your kids explore ways to support each other in their efforts to share their faith.

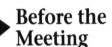

Before the Meeting

Gather a treat to share in activity 2 and enough copies of *The Youth Bible* for each student.

1. Mark's Story

Read aloud the devotion, "Why Didn't You Say Something?" and the accompanying passage, Romans 10:8-18, and discuss the questions at the end of the story.

Then ask: **Why is it so hard to tell others about what we believe?**

Say: **Today we're going to see what can help us overcome our fears about sharing our faith.**

2. Something to Share

Before the session, give one of your group members a treat to share with the rest of the group, such as a pound of M&M's or something else kids will enjoy. Tell that person to enthusiastically announce and pass out the treat when you give the signal.

Say: **Someone here has something special to tell you about.**

Then give the signal to your treat person. After kids have received the treats, ask: **How did it feel to get a treat unexpectedly? How did it feel to give the treat? How would the rest of you have felt if (name of treat-giver) had decided to keep the treats? How is this like giving away your faith? How is it different?**

Say: **If we believe that our faith really means something, telling others about it is like giving them an unexpected treat. If they accept it, they'll understand how great it is. If they don't, we haven't lost a thing.**

3. Stories to Tell

Assign kids each one of the following devotions and passages: "How Can I Tell You?" Isaiah 60:1-6; "Salt and Light," Matthew 5:13-16;

"Pass It On!" Mark 16:19-20; "Unknown Soldiers," Luke 10:1-12; "Responding to Opportunities," Acts 4:1-13; "Giving It All," 1 Corinthians 9:16-27; or "What to Say?" 2 Timothy 1:3-14. (You don't need to use all the devotions and passages.)

Have kids pair off with someone who doesn't have the same devotion. After they've silently read their devotion and passage, they'll explain what they read to their partner.

Then have pairs work together to come up with answers to the questions in their devotions. Once they've discussed the questions, have pairs each find another pair with different devotions. The four kids will sit down together and, as pairs, explain their two devotions to the other pair.

Give foursomes about five minutes to discuss their devotions. Then bring everyone together and have one person from each foursome report the group's findings. Be sure kids tell what their scripture passage had to say about sharing faith.

Then ask: **How did it feel telling your part-ner about your devotion? How did it feel when your pair told another pair about your devotions? How is this like telling others about our faith? How can we support each other in telling our friends about our faith like we supported our partners in this activity?**

Say: **The Bible gives us encouragement and ways to share our faith. And we can give each other support just like the partners gave each other support as we shared together in our foursomes.**

▶ 4. Fearless Foursomes

Have your kids return to their groups of four to examine the "Consider ..." sections of their original devotions. Have each person choose one idea to act on and share it with the rest of the group. Then have the others tell what they will do to support that person's efforts.

Close your session by having kids pray together in their groups.

THE TRUTH ABOUT THE COMMON COLD

THEME: Sickness

▶ Before the Meeting

Gather a die, a marker, newsprint, pens and blank stationery. Make sure everyone has a copy of *The Youth Bible*.

Sickness was never God's plan for us. Illness and death are both the result of living in a fallen world that's waiting for redemption from the effects of human sin. But God's given us ways—through doctors and through divine healing—to overcome illness even while we live in this world. This meeting helps kids understand why people get sick and how to handle illness when it comes.

▶ 1. The Germ-Giver

Set up a circle of chairs using about six more chairs than there are players. Have kids stand outside the circle.

Say: **Pretend this circle is a sort of game board. I'll choose one of you to act as the Carrier, and the rest of you will be Potential Victims. The disease the Carrier has instantly kills whoever contracts it, though the Carrier remains unaffected.**

Have kids all gather behind you. Designate a starting point on the circle and make an opening there where kids can enter and exit. Have the Carrier you've chosen sit in the chair to the left of the opening. Kids will enter the circle one by one and roll a die to see how many chairs they progress clockwise. After each person's roll, the Carrier always moves three chairs clockwise, while the person who rolled the die and the players already in the circle will move ahead the number of chairs determined by the roll.

Any person who ends up on the space the Carrier occupies dies instantly and leaves the game. Players who make it all the way around the circle can exit the game and are safe. When all players are either dead or safe, you can start over with a new Carrier.

Continue play for five or 10 minutes until several people have died.

After the game, ask: **How did you like this game? How did it feel to die while others lived? How do your feelings compare with** those of people in real life who have fatal diseases?

Say: **Today we're going to discuss disease—where it comes from and how it fits into our beliefs as Christians.**

 ## 2. The Word on Sickness

Form four groups. Assign each group one of the following passages from *The Youth Bible*: 2 Kings 5:1-14; Matthew 9:35—10:8; Mark 5:21-43; or Mark 7:31-37. Have groups each read their passage, then draw from it ideas on God's perspective on sickness. When groups are finished, have them each tell what they discovered. Write kids' responses on newsprint.

Then ask: **Why does God allow disease? According to these passages, what are some good things that came out of disease?**

 ## 3. Hope-Givers

Ask four volunteers to read aloud the devotions in *The Youth Bible* related to the scripture passages kids just studied. The devotions are:

"Take Your Medicine" (p. 337), "Giving the World Friends" (p. 924), "Miracles Happen" (p. 973) and "She Made a Difference" (p. 978).

After the reading, distribute stationery and pens and ask kids each to write a letter of hope, encouragement or admiration to one of the four people described in the devotions. Tell kids to base their letters on what they've just learned about dealing with sickness. Allow about 10 minutes, then ask for volunteers to read what they wrote. Applaud kids' efforts.

Then say: **We may never understand all of God's ways when it comes to sickness, but we can believe that he's working out things for the best. And we can always pray for the sick. Let's close today by praying for those we know who need God's touch.**

 ## 4. Prayer-Givers

Ask kids to tell their concerns for friends and family who are ill. Then have kids return to their study groups from activity 2 and take turns praying for each other's requests.

Dismiss kids as they finish praying.

THE DEVIL MADE ME DO IT?

THEME: Sin

Sinning to solve a problem or to meet a need in our lives is like trying to get rid of a hole in the ground by digging it out. The more you dig, the bigger the hole gets. Sometimes kids don't understand that even the "harmless" sins they dabble in now can lead to much more damaging sins in the future. This meeting helps kids see the long-term damaging effects of sin and discover and act on God's "sin solutions" in the Bible.

▶ Before the Meeting

Stack all the chairs against the wall at one end of the room. Gather a large garbage bag with tie handles for each group member, a stack of newspapers, newsprint and a marker. Stack copies of *The Youth Bible* at the other end of the room.

▶ 1. Stuff It

As kids arrive, give them each a garbage bag and a stack of newspapers and have them sit on the floor.

Say: **Think of one sin or bad thing you've done in your life. Then pull out a sheet of newspaper, crumple it and stuff it in your garbage bag. Keep stuffing "sins" into your bag until it's at least half full.**

When the bags are looking pretty well stuffed, call time. Have kids each tie the top of their garbage bag around one ankle.

Say: **Now I'd like everyone to get a chair** and a copy of *The Youth Bible*. **Let's set up the chairs in a circle.**

After kids have struggled to drag their bags and get the room set up, say: **You guys were awfully slow. What's the problem?**

Ask: **How did it feel dragging around your bag of sins as you set up the room? How is this like what sin does to us in real life?**

Say: **Today we're going to look at what sin is, what it does to us and what the Bible tells us to do about it.**

▶ 2. Asking for Trouble

Kids may be ready to get rid of their bags by now, but explain that sin isn't that easy to get rid of—that they'll have to wear the bags for most of the meeting.

Have kids form three groups. Assign each group one of the following devotions and passages from *The Youth Bible*: "An Expensive

CD," Genesis 3:8-24; "I Told You So," Exodus 32:1-14; or "Unfair Acquisitions," Malachi 4:1-2.

Say: **Sometimes we sin in a big way, knowing right from the start that what we're doing is wrong. Read through your devotion and passage. Then be prepared to tell the group about your character's sin, the consequences and the solution the Bible passage offers.**

Allow a few minutes for study and discussion. Then bring groups together and have them share their findings. As kids share their solutions from the Bible, record them on newsprint.

▶ 3. Subtle Sin

Say: **Many of us never plan to do wrong— sin just kind of creeps up on us.**

Have kids return to their groups and read one of the following devotions and passages from *The Youth Bible*: "What Harm?" Psalm 130; "Laughing at Others' Troubles," Obadiah 12-14; or "Unexpected Forgiveness," Hebrews 9:11-28.

Say: **Prepare to share with the rest of us how your character got into subtle sin, how he or she could have prevented the problem and what "sin solutions" the Bible passage offers.**

After a few minutes of study and discussion, bring everyone together and have groups share their findings once more. Again, record the sin solutions on newsprint.

▶ 4. Quiet Reflection

Say: **Maybe one of these devotions you've studied or heard about has reminded you of a sin problem in your life. I'd like you to spread out around the classroom, separate yourselves from each other, bow your heads quietly and talk to God about any sin problems you might have in your life.**

After a minute of silence, choose one of these devotions from *The Youth Bible* to read aloud: "Taking the Weight Off" (p. 660) or "Hidden Sins" (p. 285). Then read aloud Isaiah 43:18-19, 25.

▶ 5. Sin Stomp

Say: **There's no more wonderful feeling in the world than getting rid of the sin in our lives.**

Have kids untie their garbage bags and pile all the crumpled newspapers in the center of the room. Then have them stomp on the crumpled papers and stuff them into as few garbage bags as possible.

Ask: **How does it feel to be free of your bag of sins? How does that feeling compare to being truly free of sin in your heart? How does our method of getting rid of sins (stomping them and stuffing them in bags) compare to God's method?**

Close with prayer, thanking God for the joy of a clean heart and for his free gift of forgiveness.

HOW DOES YOUR GARDEN GROW?

THEME: Spiritual Growth

Being a Christian is most rewarding when we're bearing fruit for God's kingdom. Throughout the Bible, real people just like us learned what it meant to grow spiritually and make every day count for God. Use this meeting to introduce your kids to principles of spiritual growth that will help them mature and bear fruit as Christians.

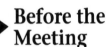

Before the Meeting

Bring an ailing potted plant and containers of salt and vinegar. Gather paper, pencils, newsprint, markers, a bunch of grapes, seed packets, business card-size slips of paper, a shovel and a small tree to plant in the church yard (make sure you get permission to plant it). Obtain a copy of *The Youth Bible* for each student.

▶ 1. Plant Doctor

Display the ailing plant, pretending to be a concerned gardner.

Say: **My plant isn't growing like I want it to. I've tried all these things on it, and I've kept it in a dark room. But it just won't grow.**

Show kids the salt and vinegar you've supposedly used on the plant.

Ask: **What do you think is wrong? Why won't my plant grow?**

Kids will probably say you don't have the right conditions for growth.

Say: **Just as this plant needs the right conditions for growth, Christians also need the right conditions to grow spiritually.**

Form five groups. Assign each group one of the following devotions and passages from *The Youth Bible*: "Wrestling With God," Genesis 32:22-32; "Who Am I?" Luke 2:41-52; "Every Day Counts," Luke 13:1-9; "Cheri's Gift," John 15:1-17; or "Living for God," Romans 8:6-17.

Distribute paper and pencils. Have groups each list conditions for spiritual growth using their devotion, scripture and "For More, See ..." passages.

▶ 2. Weed Eaters

As groups are working, list the following "weeds" on a sheet of newsprint: doubt, resisting God, laziness, fear, selfishness, greed and refusing to use talents.

Ask: **How do these "weeds" affect our spiritual lives the way real weeds affect a flourishing plant?**

Have groups look at their lists from activity 1 and decide which weeds the conditions on their lists could get rid of. Bring everyone together and have kids share their findings.

3. Fruitfully Yours

Have volunteers read aloud 1 Thessalonians 1:1-10 and the related devotion, "Spreading Love Around." Discuss the questions at the end. Then display a luscious bunch of grapes.

Ask: **What comparisons can you make between this bunch of grapes and Christians who are living fruitful lives for God?**

Pass the grapes around. Have each person take one, and then give one idea for becoming more fruitful personally or as a youth group.

4. Sowing Seeds

When the cluster of grapes gets back to you, say: **When our lives begin to bear fruit for God, everyone benefits. But the fruit that** we enjoy—both spiritually and physically— is the result of a long process of carefully tended growth. In our spiritual lives, that process begins with seeds of faith and obedience.

Distribute packets of seeds with business card-size slips of paper taped to them. Have kids each look at the "Consider . . ." sections of their devotions and write on their seed packet one thing they'll do this week to help them grow spiritually.

5. Keep Growing

Show kids the small tree you brought to plant in the church yard. Take the group outside and have kids help dig the hole and carefully place the tree in it. Have other kids water the tree and gently tamp the soil in place around the roots.

Stand in a circle around the tree.

Say: **This tree will be a symbol of our spiritual growth in this group. As you watch it grow, be reminded to watch for spiritual growth in your own life and in the lives of others in the group.**

Ask a volunteer to close in prayer.

WHEN IT HURTS

THEME: Suffering

Suffering is definitely not something you would wish on anybody. Yet we find that throughout history, the people who rocked their world were the people who were trained in the school of suffering. This session will help your kids get beyond the whys of suffering to the more essential question of: What is God teaching me through this?

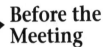

Before the Meeting

Gather materials to make two life-size male dummies. You'll need crumpled newspaper or fiberfill for stuffing; a nice suit, white shirt and tie for one dummy; and scruffy work clothes for the other. Heads can be made of balls or balloons with wigs or mops on top.

You'll also need pencils, 3×5 cards, a small box, giftwrap, ribbon, a small bow, newsprint, a marker and a copy of the *The Youth Bible* for each group member.

1. Who's This Dummy?

Form two groups. Assign one group the task of making "Mr. Stuffy"—a privileged, prosperous dummy who has never suffered in any way; the other group will make a "Joe Less-Than-Average"—a poor, suffering dummy whose life has had more downs than ups.

Say to both groups: **As you construct your dummy, I want you to develop an identity for him. Give him a personal history, a family, a job, hobbies, possessions and a personality.**

When the groups have finished their work, have them prop their dummies on chairs at the front of the room. Give each group an opportunity to introduce their dummy.

Then ask: **What characteristics is Joe Less-Than-Average likely to have that Mr. Stuffy won't? Which of these dummies would probably make a better friend? Explain. How do you think their understanding of God would differ?**

2. Life Is Like That

Have kids count off by threes to form groups. Assign each group one of the following devotions and passages from *The Youth Bible*: "Running for His Life," Exodus 1:6—2:10; "In Sickness and in Health ..." Isaiah 63:7-9; or

186

"Lord, Remember Me," Lamentations 3:1-24.

Have groups read through their devotion and passage and discuss the questions at the end. Then bring everyone together.

Ask each group: **Whose fault was it that your character suffered? What does your passage teach about suffering? Did the character reflect the attitude described? Explain.**

▶ 3. Hard Choices

Say: **Sometimes people suffer just because life dishes out difficult circumstances. But sometimes our suffering is brought on by choices we make—even if they are good choices.**

Have kids re-form their groups of three. Assign each group a second devotion and passage from *The Youth Bible*. Include: "The Price of Goals," Luke 22:63-71; "When a Dream Dies," 2 Thessalonians 1:1-12; and "The Cost of Faith," 1 Peter 4:12-19. Have kids read and discuss the devotion, passage and questions.

Then bring everyone together and ask each group: **How was personal choice involved in your character's suffering? What were the benefits of his suffering? Would you have made the same choices he did? Explain.**

▶ 4. Personal Pain

Distribute pencils and 3×5 cards. Have kids space themselves out in the room for maximum privacy.

Ask: **What's the hardest experience you ever lived through? Maybe there are two or three really painful times that stand out in your mind. Jot them down on your card.**

Give kids a moment to reflect and write.

Then ask: **What did you learn about God** from that experience? about yourself? about life? Write brief answers to these questions on the other side of your card. If you haven't figured it all out yet, write a question mark.

Ask for volunteers who would feel comfortable sharing their painful experiences and the insights they gained.

▶ 5. Precious Moments

Gather all the cards in a small box. As kids watch, and without saying anything, wrap the box in beautiful gift wrap and add a ribbon and bow. If you're all thumbs at gift-wrapping, have a couple of volunteers help out. Place the wrapped box in front of the kids and read Isaiah 63:7-9 out loud.

Say: **Sometimes when we're in the midst of a hurtful situation it feels like God has just forgotten about us and left us dangling in a mess. But we know from God's Word that just the opposite is true. I gift-wrapped these cards to show that the times when we suffer can be some of the most precious times in our lives. What are some of the gifts we receive when we suffer?**

List kids' responses on a sheet of newsprint.

Have kids return to their groups of three. Encourage kids to share within their groups things that are causing them pain, and to pray for each other. Be sensitive to kids who may not be willing to share their pain publicly but could benefit from private words of encouragement and support.

Have kids gather around the gift-wrapped box and touch it with one hand as you close in prayer. Lead kids in thanking God for the good things that come from the hurtful times in our lives, for a savior who understands, and for friends who care.

TWO LITTLE WORDS

THEME: Thankfulness

It's easy for any of us to get caught in the trap of wanting more and more things and being less and less satisfied with what we have. And teenagers are no exception. But we all have lots to thank God for, if we only force ourselves to stop and think about it. Use this session to help your kids see why they should express thanks to God and how they can do it.

▶ Before the Meeting

Gather newsprint or a chalkboard, a marker, pencils, paper and a copy of *The Youth Bible* for each student.

▶ 1. Thankful Greeting

As kids arrive, greet them each personally, thanking them for coming and giving them each at least one sincere compliment. For example, you might say, "Thanks for coming Maria; I really appreciate your faithfulness."

After everyone has arrived, say: **I really meant what I said as I greeted you today. How did it feel to be thanked? How did it feel when I complimented you? How might that be like how God feels when we express our thankfulness to him?**

Say: **God isn't human like we are, but he enjoys the thankfulness of his people. To**day we're going to look at some new ways of expressing **our thankfulness to him.**

▶ 2. Why Be Thankful?

Have a group member read aloud Deuteronomy 8:10-18 from *The Youth Bible*. Then have someone else read the accompanying devotion, "Remembering Love."

Ask: **Why should we be thankful to God? How did God help Terrence and his family? What other responses besides thankfulness could Terrence have had? What has God done for you or for your family?**

▶ 3. Memories for the Thanks

Say: **God has done so much for us that it should be natural for us to be thankful. But sometimes it's not so easy. Let's look**

at examples of modern people and Bible characters who found particular reasons for giving thanks.

Form two teams. Write the following devotions and passages on a chalkboard or newsprint: "Unnoticed Gifts," 2 Samuel 7:18-29; "A Letter to Dad," 1 Chronicles 29:10-13; "Thanks, But No Thanks," Psalm 116; "A Simple Thank You," Jonah 2:2-9; and "Attitude of Gratitude," Luke 17:11-19.

Have teams each divide up the devotions among their team members and study the devotions, passages and questions for five to 10 minutes.

Then line teams up facing each other, about 4 feet apart. Have the first person on team one shout out something to be thankful for. Then give the first person on team two five seconds to shout something else to thank God for that begins with the same letter. For example, if the team one person said, "parents," the person on team two could say, "power."

If the person on team two shouts out something beginning with the same letter within five seconds, team two gets 100 points and the next person on team two continues the game by shouting out something else to be thankful for. If the team two person doesn't shout something appropriate in time, team one gets 100 points and the next person on team one continues the game. Move on to the next letter whenever someone fails to shout a word within five seconds.

Remind kids to think about the passages and devotions for ideas. Almost anything is acceptable, as long as it's something we can thank God for. Don't allow any repeats.

Keep going until everyone has had at least one chance at yelling something out. Go through the kids twice if you have fewer than 12.

Ask: **How did it feel when someone on your team shouted out an answer in time? How did it feel when someone didn't get an answer out in time? How might that be like the way God feels when we thank him or when we fail to thank him?**

▶ **4. Acting in Thanks**

Gather kids back into one group.

Say: **We've come up with a bunch of things to be thankful for; now we're going to do something about them.**

Choose six kids to read aloud the "Consider . . ." sections from the six devotions studied in this session. Encourage the rest of the kids to listen carefully and choose one idea they can act on immediately. Have paper and pencils available for kids who choose to do writing activities.

Allow about five minutes for kids to complete their work. Encourage those who aren't finished to do the rest of the activity at home this week.

▶ **5. Thanks, God**

Form a circle for prayer. Have volunteers pray sentence prayers, starting with "Thanks, God, for . . ." (It's best to go in random order so kids who feel uncomfortable praying aloud don't feel forced to do so.) Close with your own prayer of thanks and an "amen."

FROM WORRY TO SECURITY

THEME: Worry

What if the world comes to an end?
What if my parents get a divorce?
What if no one ever loves me enough to marry me?
What if I don't make good enough grades for college?
What if I get a disease no one can cure?
All teenagers spend at least some of their time worrying. This meeting helps kids stop worrying about things they can't control and start trusting in the one who controls everything.

▶ Before the Meeting

Gather several hymnals or heavy books, paper, pencils, newsprint and markers. Make sure everyone has a copy of *The Youth Bible*.

▶ 1. The Pile-On

Put a stack of hymnals or heavy books in the front of the room. Ask for a volunteer to be a temporary "worry wart."

Say: **We're going to rename these books to represent terrible things that might happen to our worry wart. Each time we name a book, we'll hand it to (name) to add it to (his or her) pile of worries.**

Examples of book titles might include: *World War Three*, *The House Fire*, *The Terrible Car Wreck* and *Invasion of the Space Monsters*. Encourage kids to be creative as they pile up the volunteer with all kinds of imaginary worries. Keep the process going until the worry wart can barely hold the books.

Say: **(Name), you look pretty worried. But I've got some bad news.** Bring out a huge dictionary or encyclopedia and place it on top of the pile.

Say: **This is called** *The Day the Sky Fell*.

As you place the last book on the pile, push down just enough to cause the volunteer to drop everything. Make sure no one is in close enough range to get a broken limb in the collapse.

Ask: **How did it feel to be piled up with all those worries? How was piling up (name) with real and imaginary worries like what we do to ourselves in real life? How was "the collapse" like what happens to people who worry all the time?**

Say: **We all worry about things from time to time. But God doesn't want us to be victims of constant worry. Today we're going to see what the Bible teaches about how to handle our worries.**

2. Worry Letters

Distribute paper and pencils. Have kids each write an anonymous letter asking advice about a specific worry they face. Explain that kids should make their letters specific but not include anything that would identify anyone, including themselves.

When everyone is finished, collect the letters and keep them until later in the session.

Say: **Sometimes our own worries seem huge in our minds. Let's look at the stories of modern and Bible-time people and see what kinds of worries they confronted and how they responded.**

3. If They Can, I Can

Form three groups. Assign each group two of the following devotions and passages from *The Youth Bible*: "A Little Hope," Exodus 16:2-15; "Geronimo-o-o-o!" Psalm 62; "Sweating It Out," Matthew 6:25-34; "Making It Through Your Day," Matthew 11:25-30; "First Letter Home," Luke 10:38-42; "Let It Rain!" Romans 8:31-39; and "Weighty Worries," 1 Peter 5:6-11.

Have groups read their devotions and passages and discuss the questions at the end. Then bring everyone together and have groups report what they learned from the stories and scripture passages about handling worry. Record kids' ideas on newsprint.

Say: **Now that we have general guidelines for dealing with worries, let's use our knowledge to tackle the worry you wrote about in your letters.**

4. Answers From God

Distribute the letters kids wrote in activity 2. Have kids read aloud the letter they were handed. Have the whole group brainstorm ways to deal with the worry described in the letters. Encourage kids to support their ideas with the scripture they studied.

5. Worry-fetti

To close, have kids take their letters and shred them into tiny pieces. On the count of three, have kids throw their confetti into the air as a sign of giving their worries over to God.

Declare that kids are officially "worry-free" and encourage them to stay that way for the rest of their lives.

Ask volunteers to help you pick up the confetti so you don't cause any worries for the person who cleans your church.

WITH MY WHOLE HEART

THEME: Worship

Worship, to a lot of kids, means Sunday morning church. Some of them have never experienced a "Wow!" moment of spontaneous appreciation for God and his creation. This meeting is designed to allow your kids to explore the whys and hows of worship and to discover that, in the end, everything they do is potentially an act of worship.

▶ Before the Meeting

Gather cassette tapes of various styles of worship music, a cassette player, newsprint and markers. Make sure each group member has a copy of *The Youth Bible*.

▶ 1. Sweet, Sweet Songs

Open with a couple of your kids' favorite worship songs.

Ask: **How do you feel when we sing these songs? What makes a good worship song?**

Play short excerpts of other types of worship music on cassette.

After each one, ask: **How does this type of music make you feel? In what setting would this music be appropriate? Does it help you worship?**

Say: **Music is just one aspect of the larger topic of worship we're going to be discuss-**ing today. Obviously, worship is a very personal thing, as we saw with these different styles of music. **There is something more important than style to consider in worship, however. Let's find out what that is.**

▶ 2. Why Worship?

Have kids turn to the devotion "1964" (p. 987 in *The Youth Bible*). Have a volunteer read it aloud. Then read aloud the related scripture passage, Mark 11:1-11.

Ask: **What kinds of things do people worship today with the same enthusiasm shown in "Beatlemania"? Have you ever seen people get as excited about God as they do about their favorite sporting event? Is it appropriate to show that kind of enthusiasm in worship? Explain.**

▶ 3. Worship in the Bible

Form groups of three or more. Assign two of the following devotions and passages from *The Youth Bible* to each group: "Clapping, Shouting, Singing," Psalm 47; "Happy Are Those," Psalm 84; "Time Out!" Psalm 150; "Understanding God's Heart," Isaiah 6:1-8; "Awesome Stuff," Luke 2:8-21; "Remember Me?" 1 Corinthians 11:23-26; "Why Doesn't God Talk?" Hebrews 12:18-25; "Worship's Many Faces," Revelation 5:11-14. (You don't have to use all the passages.)

Say: **As you read through your devotions and passages, I want you to look for answers to these two questions: Why did these people worship? What can we learn about worship from their experiences?**

After groups have read and discussed their devotions and passages, bring everyone together and have groups share their findings. Record their ideas about worship on a large sheet of newsprint.

Ask: **Why do you think God wants us to worship? How does worship help us?**

▶ 4. Wow!

Have kids turn to the devotion "Enjoying God's Gifts" (p. 908 in *The Youth Bible*). Read it aloud, then discuss the questions at the end.

Ask: **What brings us to the moment of "Wow!" in worship? What's the neatest worship experience you can remember?**

Say: **I want you to return to the groups you were with in activity 3. Your task is to** plan a worship service. It can be as crea- **tive as you like. You can use any setting. Your object will be to bring the people who participate to that moment of "Wow!" where they truly appreciate who God is and what he has done.**

Explain that groups will have 10 minutes to plan their worship experience. There are no restrictions—they can be completely creative. Encourage them to refer to the worship ideas listed on the newsprint.

After 10 minutes, bring the groups together and have them share their worship plans. You may wish to have kids synthesize several of their ideas into a worship service for the entire congregation.

▶ 5. A New Song

Have kids turn to Psalm 150. Put up a large sheet of newsprint.

Say: **"Praise him with loud, crashing cymbals" probably works just as well today as it did two centuries ago, but harps and lyres may be a bit out of date. How could we rewrite this psalm to reflect today's culture?**

It will be easier to pull ideas from kids if you have them suggest individual lines for a modern psalm which you later pull into logical sequence. Encourage kids to finish the sentence, "Praise God with ..."

Assemble the finished psalm as a choral reading and close the meeting by having kids perform it.

193

SIDELIGHT GAMES AND ACTIVITIES

Was Eve's fateful bite taken from an apple? How many football fields would fit in the ark? Did you know that Moses had the first waterbed in the Bible?

The Sidelights in *The Youth Bible* are filled with fascinating facts like these that capture kids' interest and increase their understanding and enjoyment in Bible reading. This section is filled with action-packed games and activities based on the information in the Sidelights.

Some activities are based on specific themes—others can be adapted to fit a wide range of topics. Use them at parties, to wind up and reinforce a unit of study, or as productive time-eaters anytime your youth group is together.

1. Baloney

This game will get your kids digging into their Bibles and prove once and for all which members of your group are really full of baloney.

Distribute pencils and 3×5 cards. Have kids each choose one Sidelight that interests them. Kids will take turns announcing their topic. For example, a person might say, "My Sidelight is about Solomon's Temple." The person who announced the topic will write down actual information from the Sidelight on his or her card. Other kids will make up false information about the Temple and write it down on their cards.

The person who announced the topic will collect the cards, shuffle them and read them one by one. Kids will vote on which card contains authentic information from the Sidelight.

If a made-up card gets the most votes, the person who wrote it gets a prize—a slice of bologna.

2. I Smell a Rat

No, this has nothing to do with sniffing tennis shoes.

Kids sit in a circle and scan *The Youth Bible* for interesting Sidelights. They each take turns reading a Sidelight just as it's written, or altering the facts slightly to make the Sidelight untrue.

After each Sidelight is read, take a vote. If kids smell a rat—think the sidelight has been altered to make it untrue—they wrinkle their noses and sniff the air. Kids who think the Sidelight was true give a thumbs up sign.

After the vote, the reader announces whether it was really true or false. Kids who voted correctly get a piece of M&M's candy.

3. A Zillion Questions

This game creates a small but meaningful identity crisis for each person in your group.

Write out several Sidelights on sheets of paper and tape one paper to each person's back. Kids each have to guess what their Sidelight is about by asking questions that can be answered with "yes" or "no."

If kids seem stumped about how to begin, encourage them to ask questions such as, "Am I found in the Old Testament?" "Do I refer to a person? an event? a geographical location?"

4. Buildings, Towers and Walls, Oh My!

How many rats in a ziggurat? When is a hole in a roof a real let-down? Where was a foot in the door punishable by death? Your kids will know the answers to these and other important questions after playing this game.

Form two teams. Divide the Bible in half at the beginning of Psalms. Have one group search through Sidelights about buildings, towers and walls in the first half of the Bible. Have the other search through the second half. Then have each group compile fascinating facts from their studies. The group with the most facts wins.

Now it's time to get physical. Make sure you have an equal number of kids on each team. Lead them to a soft carpet or grassy surface.

Say: **When I say "go," you have thirty seconds to create a tower using only the bodies on your team. The team with the tallest tower wins. Go!**

Creative thinkers will realize that one person standing on another's shoulders will give the greatest height in the shortest time. But don't give this secret away and spoil all the fun!

5. Bible Jeopardy

Invite parents and church staff members to join this game and share (or bare) their knowledge of Bible trivia. The adults will be amazed and delighted at the information your kids have picked up from the Sidelights in *The Youth Bible*.

Announce the event a month in advance so everyone has time to bone up. Get a creative committee together to help you set up the game. (Better yet, have kids suggest a category and a clue each time you come across a Sidelight in *The Youth Bible*.) Choose five categories. Here are some suggestions:

- Names
- People
- Construction/Buildings
- Communication
- Money
- Animals
- Geography
- Clothes/Jewelry
- Customs/Traditions
- War/Military

Choose five Sidelights from each category. On construction paper, write out a clue that could trigger a Jeopardy-style question from the contestants. Use a different color of construction paper for each of the categories.

Tape the clues face-down to a wall in five columns with the category heading at the top. Number the clues in each category from top to bottom.

Form two teams. Set a table in front of the game wall. Each team sends one player at a time to the table. Players take turns asking for a category and a number. You pull the paper off and read the clue. If a player asks the right question, his or her team gets 10 points. If the player's question is incorrect, the other team's player gets a shot at the question and the 10 points.

6. Sidelight Charades

Get everyone into the act!

Challenge kids to find an interesting Sidelight, then act it out and have other kids guess the topic. The Sidelight on David drooling and acting the fool (1 Samuel 21:12-15) would be great for starters.

7. Ark Antics

Go overboard with the fun and excitement of this game.

Read the Sidelight on Genesis 6:15. Then take kids outside and measure off the dimensions of the ark. Use stakes at the corners and make chalk lines by dribbling flour from a hole cut in the corner of a flour bag.

Once you've made your ark, do animal relays—two by two, of course. Form two teams. Have kids in each team form pairs by tying arms or legs together. Have pairs "animal" to the opposite end of the ark, then run back to the starting point and tie the next pair together. Animal imitations in the race could include a duck walk, crab walk, elephant trudge, kangaroo hop, snake slither, bird flap and frog hop.

Serve animal crackers after the race.

8. Klutz Baseball

If you couldn't hit a pitched ball with a mattress, at least this game will give you an excuse.

Have kids read the Sidelight about the left-handed sharpshooters in Judges 20:16. Then set up a game of klutz baseball. It's played with a fat bat and foam ball and follows all the rules of regular baseball except that everyone plays one-handed with the hand they don't normally use.

Play as many innings as you can stand. Then top off the meeting with klutz sundaes. Have teams sit facing each other. Put bowls of ice cream and various toppings in the center of the table. Have kids create their own sundaes, then feed the person facing them, all using their off hand.

9. Dastardly Disguises

Your kids will take dastardly delight in the revenge of the sexes.

Read about Jacob's great impersonation of his twin brother in the Sidelight on Genesis 27:14-29. Then have the guys make up the girls to look like Esau.

Now turn the tables. Read about wicked Queen Jezebel in the Sidelight on 2 Kings 9:30-32. Have the girls make up the guys to look like the wicked queen.

Be sure to take a group picture before kids reassume their normal identities.

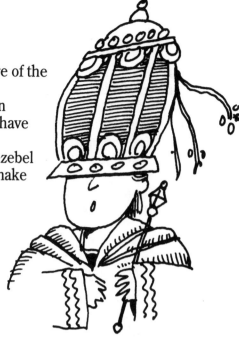

10. Header Basketball

Most guys would decline the opportunity to go one on one with Goliath. But David had a secret weapon—and it wasn't the shoes!

Have kids read the Sidelight on 1 Samuel 17:41-54. Then set up a game of header basketball. Use a foam ball (wet, if you want things to get sloppy). Mark an X at both ends of the court. One person from each team stands on the X at opposite ends of the court. Goals are scored by hitting the goal-person in the head.

Tape off a 5-foot safety zone around the goal-person. No one may enter it. The goal-person may duck, but may not move off the X or use hands to block shots.

Teams move the ball by passing only—no steps or dribbling when they're holding the ball. Kids will try to defend their goal by batting down the ball or intercepting passes. Score two points for each shot that hits the goal-person in the head. Once a goal person has been hit, kids rotate positions and a new goal-person takes over.

Although it's hard to get dangerous with a foam ball, encourage goal-persons who wear glasses to take them off.

SPLOOSH!

11. Wild Drivers

How about an off-the-road and off-the-wall chariot race? King Jehu sets the pace for this game. But stand back—drivers in this race don't have to be 16 or sane.

Have kids read the Sidelight about King Jehu's wild driving in 2 Kings 9:20. Then set up chariot teams of three kids. You'll need a slick floor and a large towel for each team. Use chairs or pylons to set an oval course. (If you really want to get crazy, make it a figure eight.)

The driver sits on the towel. The other two team members serve as horses by pulling on the front corners of the towel and dragging the driver around the course. If you have more than a dozen kids, you'll probably want to run the race in heats, then do a final run-off.

12. Bag the Flags

Robbers, rescuers and derring-do make this a great game to play outside in the dark at a lock-in or retreat.

Have kids turn in *The Youth Bible* to Luke 10:30 and read the Sidelight about the dangers of the Jericho road.

Then say: **Tonight we're going to simulate this dangerous journey.**

Form two teams. Choose someone to help you referee. Designate places at opposite ends of your boundaries as Jerusalem and Jericho. Have the traveler team wait in the church while the robber team hides in various places between Jerusalem and Jericho. Give travelers each a flag (a bandanna or rag) to wear sticking out of a back pocket or tucked into the back of their waist.

The object is for the travelers to get from Jerusalem to Jericho with their flag intact. The robbers will try to steal the flags from the travelers. Robbers can also freeze travelers if two of them tag a traveler at the same time. The traveler stays frozen until another traveler comes along and "unfreezes" him or her. After tagging a traveler, robbers must stand still and yell "one thousand one,

one thousand two, one thousand three" before chasing anyone else. Any robber who fails to do this is eliminated from the game by a referee.

Tally the number of flags that make it to Jericho in five minutes. Then have teams switch roles. The team that succeeds in getting the most flags to Jericho wins.

▶ 13. Yo—Hello!

Friendly, unique and slightly off-the-wall. If that defines your group, this activity is for you.

Have kids read the Sidelight on Paul's greeting in 2 Corinthians 1:2. Then put fertile minds together to come up with a customized greeting and handshake for your group.

You may want to have kids work in groups, then combine ideas from all the groups for the official handshake. Encourage creativity and finesse. Have everyone use the handshake as your official group greeting on all occasions, and be sure to teach it to newcomers.

Tackle important issues in the lives of your teenagers with **Active Bible Curriculum®**. Help your teenagers learn the Bible and discover how to apply it to their daily lives. And save your church money—each book includes a complete teachers guide, handout masters you can photocopy, publicity helps, and bonus ideas—all for one low price.

Order today from your local Christian bookstore, or write: Group Publishing, Box 485, Loveland, CO 80539.

PUT FAITH INTO ACTION...

...with Group's **Projects With a Purpose™ for Youth Ministry.**

Want to try something different with your 7th-12th grade classes? Group's **Projects With a Purpose™ for Youth Ministry** offers four-week courses that really get kids into their faith. Each **Project With a Purpose** course gives you tools to facilitate a project that will provide a direct, purposeful learning experience. Teenagers will discover something significant about their faith while learning the importance of working together, sharing one another's troubles, and supporting one another in love...plus they'll have lots of fun! For Sunday school classes, midweek meetings, home Bible studies, youth groups, retreats, or any time you want to help teenagers discover more about their faith.

Acting Out Jesus' Parables
Strengthen your teenagers' faith as they are challenged to understand the parables' descriptions of the Christian life. Explore such key issues as the value of humility and the importance of hope.   ISBN 1-55945-147-5

Celebrating Christ With Youth-Led Worship
Kids love to celebrate. For Christians, Jesus is the ultimate reason to celebrate. And as kids celebrate Jesus, they'll grow closer to him—an excitement that will be shared with the whole congregation.   ISBN 1-55945-410-5

Checking Your Church's Pulse
Your teenagers will find new meaning for their faith with this course. Interviews with congregational members will help your teenagers, and your church, grow closer together.   ISBN 1-55945-408-3

Serving Your Neighbors
Strengthen the "service heart" in your teenagers. They'll appreciate the importance of serving others as they follow Jesus' example.   ISBN 1-55945-406-7

Sharing Your Faith Without Fear
Teenagers don't have to be great orators to share with others what God's love means to them. Teach them to express their faith through everyday actions without fear of rejection.   ISBN 1-55945-409-1

Teaching Teenagers to Pray
Watch as your teenagers develop strong, effective prayer lives as you introduce them to the basics of prayer. They'll learn how to pray with and for others.   ISBN 1-55945-407-5

Teenagers Teaching Children
Teach your teenagers how to share the Gospel with children. Through this course, your teenagers will learn more about their faith by teaching others and develop teaching skills to last a lifetime.   ISBN 1-55945-405-9

Videotaping Your Church Members' Faith Stories
Teenagers will enjoy learning about their congregation members with this exciting video project. And, they'll learn the depth and power of God's faithfulness to his people.   ISBN 1-55945-239-0

Order today from your local Christian bookstore, or write: Group Publishing, Box 485, Loveland, CO 80539.

MORE INNOVATIVE RESOURCES
FOR YOUR YOUTH MINISTRY

The Youth Worker's Encyclopedia of Bible-Teaching Ideas:
Old Testament/ New Testament

Explore the most comprehensive idea-books available for youth workers! Discover more than 350 creative ideas in each of these 400-page encyclopedias—there's at least one idea for each and every book of the Bible. Find ideas for...retreats and overnighters, learning games, adventures, special projects, parties, prayers, music, devotions, skits, and much more!

Plus, you can use these ideas for groups of all sizes in any setting. Large or small. Sunday or mid-week meeting. Bible study. Sunday school class or retreat. Discover exciting new ways to teach each book of the Bible to your youth group.

Old Testament   ISBN 1-55945-184-X
New Testament   ISBN 1-55945-183-1

Clip-Art Cartoons for Churches

Here are over 180 funny, photocopiable illustrations to help you jazz up your calendars, newsletters, posters, fliers, transparencies, postcards, business cards, announcements—all your printed materials! These fun, fresh illustrations cover a variety of church and Christian themes, including church life, Sunday school, youth groups, school life, sermons, church events, volunteers, and more! And there's a variety of artistic styles to choose from so each piece you create will be unique and original.

Each illustration is provided in three different sizes so it's easy to use. You won't find random images here...each image is a complete cartoon. And these cartoons are fun! In fact, they're so entertaining that you may just find yourself reading the book and not photocopying them at all.

Order your copy of **Clip-Art Cartoons for Churches** today...and add some spice to your next printed piece.

ISBN 1-55945-791-0

Bore No More! (For Every Pastor, Speaker, Teacher)

This book is a must for every pastor, youth leader, teacher, and speaker. These 70 audience-grabbing activities pull listeners into your lesson or sermon—and drive your message home!

Discover clever object lessons, creative skits, and readings. Music and celebration ideas. Affirmation activities. All the innovative techniques 85 percent of adult church-goers say they wish their pastors would try! (recent Group Publishing poll)

Involve your congregation in the learning process! These complete 5- to 15-minute activities highlight common New Testament Lectionary passages, so you'll use this book week after week.

ISBN 1-55945-266-8

Order today from your local Christian bookstore, or write:
Group Publishing, Box 485, Loveland, CO 80539.